Book Cover Design by Angela Alayo

First Edition 2024

Published by Phoenix ePublishing

Contents

INTRODUCTION

Have you ever found yourself in a relationship wondering why communication with your partner often breaks down, your emotions flare up, and understanding each other seems like a real challenge? Have you ever wished to have a way to navigate through your own emotions, connect deeply with your partner, and forge a relationship built on trust, empathy, and genuine connection? If these situations strike a chord with you, then you are not alone in this.

In a world filled with superficial connections, genuine relationships have become rare, leaving many of us yearning for deep and meaningful bonds. As someone who is deeply passionate about learning the intricate dynamics of human relationships, I have spent years working on understanding the world of emotional intelligence and spiritual wisdom, to explore the mechanisms that lie within the core of profound connections.

People say, *"Love is not easy"* - and it's true! Every relationship comes with its own set of challenges. Like when communication hits a snag, leading to misunderstandings and conflicts, or trust takes a hit due to betrayals or past issues. Then there's the whole intimacy dance, with changes causing tension that needs some honest discussion and understanding. Even money matters can stir up stress, and having different expectations or parenting styles can add to the mix. Balancing work and personal life? Yep, it's a real struggle too. Jealousy and insecurity might pop up, and finding quality time can be a challenge in our busy lives. Let's not forget cultural or religious differences, and the need to align personal growth paths.

These are some of the most common issues that can affect your bond with your significant other. But don't fret! Where there is a problem, there is a solution. Over the years, as I delved deeper into the science of emotional intelligence, I have realized that most issues arise due to a lack of connection with our inner selves. We understand our partner and others better once we get in sync with our own emotions. Emotional intelligence is key to that understanding and a two-word formula to deal with multifaceted relationship challenges.

People experience a transition in their bond as soon as their relationship exits the 'honeymoon phase'. Every relationship seems exciting and rosy when it's new, but with time it all seems to change. Not because you grow out of love but because of the inability to deal with the complexities of emotions. You see, emotions make life much more complicated when they are put to use without a sense of self-awareness. We spend many years of our lives thinking that we control our own emotions, but in most cases, it is the other way around. It is our emotions that often control our minds and pull the strings. From occasional spats to deep-rooted conflicts, emotions can be difficult to manage when left unchecked. This is where emotional intelligence comes into play. It opens our minds to the possibility that we can regulate our emotions through the power of understanding and awareness. Not only does emotional intelligence help us make sense of our emotions but it also contributes to the positive expression of those feelings.

"Evidence is presented that the mass suppression of emotion throughout the civilized world has stifled our growth emotionally, leading us down a path of emotional ignorance." These words by Wayne Payne from 1985, have become more relevant and poignant in recent times. While living in a society where the show of intense emotions is often seen as a weakness, we naturally learn to ignore or hide our true emotions and lead a life within the confines of enforced pragmatism. However, as humans, we are the total sum of our thoughts, values, belief systems, and emotions, so we cannot neglect the profound role feelings play in our personal and professional lives. Unless we learn to be smart about our emotional connections and use them as a source of growth, our emotions will remain an enigma and a challenge. But the good news is emotional intelligence

is not fixed genetically, and you can learn to be self-aware, motivated, empathetic, and a socially smart individual at any age. This is where this guide comes into play!

Let me introduce the culmination of my research and work in the field of emotional intelligence - "The Happy Couple Blueprint" the guide that can transform your relationship with your person and help you connect with your own emotions. In this book, I will share not only the knowledge I acquired through a varied 50-year career which led to a significant career change in my middle years to train and practice as a Life Coach and multi-specialism Therapist.

My background has given me a diverse perspective on the intricacies of human emotions and the art of managing meaningful relationships. As a certified life coach, mentor, and multi-specialism therapist, I have had the privilege and fulfilling experience of helping many people on their paths to explore their own emotional and psychological drivers, strengthen their relationships, and enrich their lives in varied ways. Through a combination of therapeutic techniques and methodologies, I have helped my clients overcome mental and emotional barriers, guided them in healing their emotional wounds, and embraced the power of emotional intelligence and their inherent wisdom.

Throughout the book, various activities and quizzes will keep you engaged and will also let you discover several important things about yourself that you may not appreciate yet. Comprised of five parts, this book is structured into 12 easy-to-read, insightful chapters, covering the overall 10 steps that make up The Happy Couple Blueprint.

We will begin with the discovery of the hidden self. Not only will you learn about the basics of emotions, but we will also look into the connection between emotional intelligence and relationships. Then, after briefly going through the components of emotional intelligence, we will unravel some effective self-awareness exercises. This chapter aims to equip you with the necessary tools and methods to create a deeper connection with yourself and your own emotions.

The chapter that follows will introduce you to the realm of emotional balance. As we often fail to recognize the emotional patterns behind our behaviors, this section will give you tips and techniques to first identify the emotions and then address the triggers behind them. Once the cause of the emotional responses is identified, it becomes easier to manage your impulses and make decisions using both your mind and your heart. As David Caruso aptly pointed out: *"Emotional intelligence is not the triumph of heart over head - it is a unique intersection of both."*

They say passion is love's blind guide and without it, every relationship is bound to fade. Therefore, Chapter 3 brings you the secrets of igniting passion from within for the relationship's success. It will give you a roadmap to unlock your individual passion to spark and keep passion for one another. From day-to-day activities to combined exercises and surprise plans, this section has all the expert-suggested insights.

Chapter 4 discovers the transformative power of empathy, focusing on its role in strengthening the bond between you and your partner. There you can learn practical strategies that go beyond surface-level understanding, creating a deeper connection built on empathy and mutual awareness. Moving forward, Chapter 5 explores the link between social skills and effective communication. Some techniques can be used to express yourself more clearly and to understand your partner better, establishing a smoother pathway for meaningful interaction within your relationship.

Chapter 6 addresses the inevitable conflicts that arise in any relationship. It offers healthy conflict resolution techniques, to transform disagreements into opportunities for growth so that tensions can be replaced with understanding and resilience. Following conflicts, Chapter 7 takes you through the art of post-conflict healing. Through its content you can learn how to rebuild and strengthen your relationship, turning challenges into stepping stones toward a more robust and enduring connection.

For those of you who are navigating the joys and challenges of parenthood, Chapter 8 provides insights into co-parenting with emotional intelligence. You will discover how to collaboratively raise children and foster a harmonious and supportive environment for your family. Chapter 9 examines the impact your relationship has on your children. These valuable insights explain the dynamics that shape their understanding of love and partnership. You will learn how to positively influence their emotional well-being and development.

In Chapter 10, the focus shifts to the significance of everyday connection. Explore practical tips for weaving moments of intimacy and connection into your daily life, ensuring that your relationship remains vibrant and fulfilling.

Chapter 11 shares the nuanced aspects of vulnerability and intimacy. From the techniques shared there, you can learn how opening up to your partner can deepen your connection, creating a space for trust, understanding, and a more profound emotional bond. Finally, Chapter 12 sums up the strategies for future-proofing your love story. From setting shared goals to adapting to life changes, this chapter equips you with the tools to ensure your relationship withstands the test of time, evolving and growing stronger with each passing milestone of your lives together.

I would encourage you to obtain the companion Workbook, as this incorporates the exercises and activities discussed in this book, with suitable prompts and journaling pages to help you focus on the stages of your journey.

To sum up, through the pages of this book, I invite you to join me on a path of self-discovery and relationship enrichment. Together we will explore the depths of emotional intelligence, uncovering the secrets to effective communication, empathetic understanding, and authentic connection. Through real-life stories, practical exercises, and ancient wisdom, you will learn how to navigate with grace the complexities of your relationship with the most important person in your life.

PART I

Unlocking your Emotional Strengths :
Emotional Intelligence Mastery

Chapter 1

DISCOVERING YOUR HIDDEN SELF

The First Step to Transformation

Imagine you are in a heated discussion with a loved one, but instead of arguing, you pause, take a breath and put yourself in their shoes. You understand their perspective and respond with kindness and compassion. When it comes to relationships, whether it is with your partner, your family or your friends, this self-discovery journey can be a game-changer. You become more emotionally intelligent, patient and forbearing, which makes you a pretty awesome person to be around. So, you can only unlock your inner strengths and master your emotions when you understand yourself better and, in this chapter, we will go through this first step of transformation!

Discovering Your Emotions: A Deep Dive

"Emotional intelligence begins with understanding your own emotions. If you do not understand and manage your own emotions, you cannot possibly understand the emotions of others." - Daniel Goleman

If you cannot understand and manage your own emotions, you are essentially trying to navigate through a maze blindfolded. You stumble, get lost and cannot possibly help others find their way either. You might react impulsively or let your feelings get the best of you during arguments, which can lead to misunderstandings and even more conflict. But it is not just about your own emotions; it is also about being there for your partner. If we can't empathize with how they are feeling, they are in a boat by themselves in stormy seas. They might feel isolated and hurt, thinking you don't care about their emotions.

Over time, this can create a gap, making it tough to connect and truly understand each other. The conflicts might pile up and you might end up feeling frustrated and resentful. And when emotional understanding is missing, it can even make you look for that connection elsewhere, which isn't good for the relationship's health.

The Connection Between EI And Relationship Success

You know those times when it feels like you and your partner are on different wavelengths, and you just cannot seem to get through to each other? Well, that is where emotional intelligence, or EI, comes into play and can make all the difference. Let's imagine you and your partner are having a cozy date night at your favorite restaurant, sharing stories and laughter. Now, EI is the magic that takes your date to the next level, making you two feel even closer. You can easily connect with each other's emotions, empathize with their feelings and communicate on a whole new level. It creates an unspoken bond that is incredibly deep.

Back in 1992, there was this longitudinal study conducted by Gottman and Levenson, who wanted to explore the role of emotional intelligence in marital relationships and satisfaction. Couples who participated in the study were assessed for their emotional intelligence and their marital experience was tracked for five years through regular interviews and surveys. The results of this study concluded that there was a positive correlation between emotional intelligence levels and marital satisfaction. The study proved that couples who had higher emotional intelligence showed better understanding towards each other's emotions and their conflict resolution capabilities were also better than the couples who had lower levels of emotional intelligence.

So, having a solid grip on your EI works as a relationship toolkit at your disposal. You can navigate through conflicts with the finesse of a seasoned mediator, defusing any tension with ease. EI brings self-regulation into the picture, like a guiding compass for your emotions. This means even during those rocky moments; you maintain emotional stability and that trust between you and your partner continues to grow stronger.

The Five Components Of EI

Emotional intelligence is fascinating - it is made up of a multifaceted set of skills that helps us navigate the complex world of human emotions. To understand EI and learn the techniques to master it, Daniel Goleman's Mixed Model of Emotional Intelligence plays a significant role. This model breaks down the whole concept of EI into five components. If a person works on each individual component separately, they can progress towards higher levels of emotional intelligence. I see these components as a journey of exploration starting from our inner self and eventually projecting outward. Let me explain this by listing all the components here!

1. Self-Awareness

The very first component is self-awareness. It is the root of our existence, whatever we think, do, say and how we communicate with others, all of it stems from our self-awareness. The more aware we are of our strengths, weaknesses, likes and dislikes, the better we get at communicating with others. It is the first step of the emotional intelligence ladder. If you climb it, you can become apt at self-regulating your emotions and thoughts (which is the next component of EI).

Think of self-awareness as the foundation of strong emotional intelligence. It is about knowing yourself inside and out. This means understanding your emotions, recognizing what triggers them and comprehending how they influence your thoughts and actions. Let's say you realized that you become overly defensive during an argument or conflict. Self-awareness allows you to recognize the causes behind it and help understand why. You share this realization with your partner, and you end up having a practical solution to the problem that would otherwise ruin your relationship. So, this awareness empowers you to address your issues and take steps to manage them effectively.

2. Self-Regulation

Once you have identified yourself, your thoughts, and your emotions, the next step is to control them. Self-regulation is all about managing your emotional impulses, especially in challenging situations. It enables you to maintain your composure and make rational decisions. Imagine a scenario where you receive criticism from your partner. With self-regulation, you can prevent a knee-jerk defensive reaction and instead respond thoughtfully, which leads to a more constructive conversation.

3. Motivation

Motivation is the driving force behind your emotional intelligence. It is the inner spark that keeps you pushing forward, whether in your personal or professional life. Motivated people are more driven to achieve their goals and are resilient in the face of setbacks. If you are motivated to lay a strong foundation of love and support with your partner, you put in effort, communicate well, and follow a targeted plan to consistently make this love grow. Your motivation and passion drive your relationship and take it to the next level. Without motivation as a pushing factor, you give up easily and don't find the courage to put in the time and work needed.

4. Empathy

Empathy is the magic ingredient that helps you connect with others on a deeper level. It is about understanding and sharing their emotions. When you are empathetic, you can truly understand what others are going through and respond with compassion. Imagine your partner's going through a tough time. With empathy, you can put yourself in their shoes, understand their feelings, and offer support and comfort.

5. Social Skills

Social skills are like the sweet fruit of emotional intelligence.

They enable you to interact effectively with others, whether it is managing relationships, resolving conflicts or building strong networks. Let's say you are discussing the future with your partner. Strong social skills allow you to communicate clearly, collaborate effectively, and inspire your partner to work together cohesively, leading to a successful life.

Imagine Emotional Intelligence as a tree. At its foundation, much like the roots that are under the ground but secretly nourishing the tree, lies "self-awareness." Rising above the ground, similar to the tree trunk which connects the inner-awareness to the external responses, is "self-regulation." "motivation" is just like the leaves of the tree, which helps its continuous growth. Whereas "empathy" is like the branches reaching outward to the environment to offer comfort to others. Lastly, "social skills" are the fruits and outcomes of the process.

Through this tree analogy, I intend to illuminate the interconnectedness of EI's facets. Each part is connected, nourishing or enhancing every single aspect positively and contributing towards the overall improvement of emotional intelligence.

And once you master the EI skill set, you become the relationship maestro! Think of all the bad fights, arguments, disagreements, and misunderstandings you had with your partner – with this newfound skill, these interactions begin to make sense. Suddenly, you start seeing the underlying reasons behind both your actions and those of your partner. And that moment of realization becomes your first step to having a happy and healthy relationship with your partner.

Climbing Up the EI Ladder

Emotional Intelligence is not innate, but rather an acquired skill set. It requires our constant efforts, learning, and patience to climb up the EI ladder. While it is necessary to understand the importance of each component of emotional intelligence, it is also crucial to look closely into the techniques, and methods required to work on self-awareness, self-regulation, motivation, empathy, and social skills. We will delve deeper into each component in the sections to come.

In this chapter, the focus will remain on "self-awareness,"

equipping you with the tools for self-exploration. Then, Chapter 2 will give you an in-depth understanding of self-regulation through "achieving a balance of emotions." Chapter 3 will offer techniques to ignite passion and keep you motivated. Following that, in Chapter 4 you will discover techniques to develop empathy. Finally, Chapter 5 is dedicated to improving your social skills. With that being said, let's move towards the first step of this ladder!

Self-Exploration and Awareness

"Self-awareness gives you the capacity to learn from your mistakes as well as your successes. It enables you to keep growing." - Lawrence Bossidy

At some point in life, you are bound to encounter a time when you are forced to face yourself and see who you really are! For me, it was a simple incident - a small disagreement with my partner, which escalated unexpectedly. In the heat of the moment, I recognized that my emotions were spiraling beyond my control. As soon as I realized this, I took a deep breath and stepped back mentally. At that moment, I acknowledged my feelings without any judgment and recognized my tendency to be overly defensive when my opinions were challenged. This moment of self-awareness became a turning point for me.

Later, when I was by myself, I did a little self-reflection and understood the deeper cause of my reaction - the fear of rejection and my innate need for validation. This realization didn't just stop there; it allowed me to explore my feelings further. Through more introspection and applying the techniques I have learned, I started addressing my own insecurities. As I became more self-aware, my relationships started to transform. So, it all stems from self-awareness, whatever you do is the extension of your being. If you are in sync with your inner self, you will be able to create a deeper and more genuine connection with your partner.

Self-Reflection Exercise: Understanding Yourself

Do you want to dive deeper into your own thoughts but do

not have a clue where to start? This is quite common, and it is totally fine. Every time I assign self-reflection tasks to my clients, they face a similar problem. I give them questions on a worksheet, designed to guide their thoughts towards areas they do not usually think about. But before you start answering, make sure to sit in a quiet place where there are no distractions and you can concentrate on your thoughts and write each answer without any judgment.

Let's start by analyzing your emotional awareness:

1. What emotions have you been feeling lately?

2. Are there any particular situations that triggered these emotions?

3. How do you react when you experience strong emotions?

Now, let's dig into your personal values:

4. What are your basic and core values in life? (e.g., honesty, compassion, creativity)

5. How do your actions and reactions align with your values?

6. When do you feel a conflict between your values and your actions?

It is time to learn about your strengths and weaknesses:

7. What are your strengths, skills, traits, or qualities that you are proud of?

8. Are there some areas in your life where you feel the need for improvement?

9. How can you use your strengths to work on those areas for improvement?

It is time to think about relationships and communication:

10. How do you choose to communicate your needs and feelings in a relationship?

11. Is there any particular communication style that you would like to change?

12. Think about a recent conversation with your partner. How did you handle it? How could you have improved your communication?

These questions serve as thought-provoking prompts, inviting you to ponder on what has been bothering you and the reasons behind your reactions. You can either write your answers down or just give them some thought. You could also record your responses in the Workbook which accompanies this book; in any case, these questions will help you unlock your inner self and give you a general perspective. It is only after gaining this insight about yourself that you can take the necessary steps towards better self-awareness.

The Power of Reflection and Journaling

"Knowing yourself is the beginning of all wisdom." Aristotle

It all begins with self-awareness; from the way we handle our emotions to the ways we react to situations. Everything starts making sense when we discover who we are. And this path to self-discovery goes through self-reflection. It allows you to look into yourself deeply and discover yourself, your beliefs, core values, and perspective. It becomes easier to control your impulses and manage your communication with others when you know where your reactions are coming from and what triggers them.

Have you ever been in a situation where you couldn't figure out why you felt a certain way? And having no answer to that question made you feel a little frustrated. It is natural. Just as it takes time to understand others, it also requires time to get to know our inner self. And the best way to accomplish that is reflection. One of the most effective techniques to self-reflect is journaling. In a research study carried out by Dr. James Pennebaker, a psychologist and researcher at the University of Texas in Austin, the power of expressive writing (a form of journaling) was brought to light.

The study explored the effects of writing about emotional experiences on psychological well-being. All the participants were asked to write about their deepest thoughts and feelings regarding a traumatic or stressful event for 15–20 minutes a day over several consecutive days.

The results? The participants who engaged in expressive writing reported significant improvements not only in their mental health but also in their physical health. They experienced fewer visits to the doctor, enhanced immune function, and an overall boost in well-being compared to the control group.

This study offers a solid nod to the therapeutic benefits of putting pen to paper. It is scientific validation for the age-old practice of journaling as a tool for processing emotions, gaining clarity, and promoting overall health.

Practicing Self-Reflection

Besides journaling, there are various other practices that you can put to use and become more self-aware. The following activities are designed to help you think deeply about your own thoughts, feelings, actions, and values.

1. What Is Your Super-Power?

This exercise is designed to help you embrace your whole self, recognizing that neither your positive qualities (Superpowers) nor your negative traits (Kryptonite) are inherently good or bad. How you use them determines their impact on your life.

To start, identify and write down one personal Superpower and one Kryptonite. For instance, my Superpower is my ability to connect seemingly unrelated ideas and my Kryptonite is impatience, which makes me anxious when people take too long to respond or act. The key takeaway here is that neither of these traits is inherently positive or negative. It is all about how we use them.

2. Morning Pages

When I first heard about the "Morning Pages" exercise proposed by Julia B. Cameron (an American author, poet, and teacher), I didn't fully comprehend its power. "How am I supposed to write anything just after waking up?" - That was my initial reaction! But once I started practicing this exercise it did wonders for me. Not only did it unlock my creativity, but it also helped me connect with my inner self and my intuition.

Through the power of this exercise, I was able to work through all the issues that were bothering me. I left situations that were not good for me, and I was able to align my priorities in life. Not to mention, it also brought me great peace of mind.

Trust me! It is a wonderfully liberating exercise that can bring a lot of benefits. Imagine starting your day with a clean mental slate. The key here is not to filter anything; it is about decluttering your mind. For this exercise, you will have to sit down and place a paper or notebook in front of you. Grab a pen and start writing whatever comes to your mind, without giving it too much thought or stopping. The purpose is to let your emotions and thoughts flow without judgment. It is ideal to write three pages per morning for this exercise. When you carry out this exercise in the morning, it lets your uncluttered mind generate a stream of ideas and thoughts that are free from external influences, allowing you to learn about your inner feelings and vision.

3. The Three Whys

The "Three Whys" is a great technique that allows you to explore the underlying causes and reasons behind a particular situation or decision by repeatedly asking "Why?" three times. This exercise was initially developed by Sakichi Toyoda and was famously used by Toyota to improve its manufacturing processes.

Think of it as a way to uncover the hidden layers of cause and effect. When you are faced with a problem or decision, you start by asking "Why?" to understand the primary reason. That would be like peeling back the first layer of an onion. Consider a scenario where you had to cancel dinner plans with your partner because of a work emergency, and despite their claim of being 'fine,' you sense otherwise. Now, instead of assuming things, try the "Three Whys" approach. Ask them, "*Why are you upset about canceling plans?*" A possible answer might be, "*Because I was looking forward to spending time together.*"

To dig deep, ask the next question, "*Why is spending time together important to you?*"

A likely response might be, "*Because it makes me feel valued and connected.*"

The answer to the third question finally reveals the deeper emotions at play. You can ask something like: "*Why does feeling valued and connected matter to you?*" To which they might respond, "*Because it strengthens our bond and I crave a deep connection in our relationship.*"

By the time you reach the third "Why?" you often arrive at a deeper understanding of the situation or decision and sometimes, you might even uncover something about yourself that you hadn't fully grasped before.

4. Meditation

Meditation works like a miracle when it comes to self-awareness. It serves as the surfboard in the vast ocean of consciousness, which allows you to navigate the waves of your thoughts, emotions, and sensations. Through the practice of meditation, you can gain insights into your own mind and emotions and foster a deep sense of self-awareness. There are different techniques that you can employ to meditate:

Walking Meditation:
You just had an argument with your partner, and you don't know what to do; take a slow walk and let your mind focus on the present moment. When practicing walking meditation, you need to pay attention to each step you take, and the way your feet lift and touch the ground. Feel the movement of your body with each step. During this walk, engage your senses fully in the process – notice the sounds, smells, and sights around you. Doing this meditation promotes awareness of your body in motion and the environment.

Body Scan Meditation:
How does this form of meditation help with self-awareness? It gives you the time and capacity to focus on yourself. You can carry out this meditation by lying down on the ground or sitting somewhere comfortably in a relaxing environment. Close your eyes and focus your attention on each part of your body at a time, starting from your toes and then moving slowly up to your head. Notice all the sensations, tension, or relaxation in all the areas. This exercise increases your awareness of physical sensations and lets you relax emotionally.

Mindful Breathing:
You are in the middle of the argument and you cannot think how to react to the situation. Just take a step back and give your mind the time to relax. Mindful breathing works like magic to calm you down and rewind. For this, find a quiet place to sit or lie down. Close your eyes and focus on your breath. Notice the sensation of the air entering and leaving your nostrils or the rise and fall of your chest and abdomen. Whenever your mind starts to wander, gently bring your focus back to your breath. This exercise helps in cultivating attention and awareness.

Chapter 2

ACHIEVING EMOTIONAL BALANCE

The Key to Personal Growth

Emotional balance is the cornerstone of personal growth. It fosters resilience, inner peace, and our overall well-being. We all have a wide range of emotions, and we need to acknowledge them without getting overwhelmed. Emotional balance does not mean that you should suppress negative feelings, but instead learn to manage them constructively. By developing emotional intelligence, you can identify, comprehend, and respond to your emotions and the emotions of others. This awareness allows for healthier interpersonal relationships, effective communication, and empathetic understanding.

Recognizing Emotional Patterns

Our emotional patterns play a major role in defining how we communicate with others, especially with our partners. Each one of us has our own set of patterns and it is by identifying these patterns we can gain the ability to anticipate our emotional responses and understand the underlying reasons behind them. This self-awareness empowers us to make conscious choices rather than being driven solely by impulsive reactions. It not only promotes emotional intelligence but also enables our personal growth and transformation. It equips us with the tools to navigate difficult situations, build healthier relationships, and cultivate a profound sense of self-acceptance.

So, how can we identify our emotional patterns? There are several ways to tap into your emotions and discover their respective triggers. For you, I have the perfect activity to assess your emotional state.

Questionnaire: Emotional Responses

To answer each of the following statements, think about your typical emotional responses and patterns in different situations and be honest with yourself!

I react strongly to even minor frustrations or disappointments.

1) Never
2) Rarely
3) Occasionally
4) Often
5) Always

I find it difficult to control my anger and temper when I am upset.

1) Never
2) Rarely
3) Occasionally
4) Often
5) Always

I often feel overwhelmed by my emotions.

1) Never
2) Rarely
3) Occasionally
4) Often
5) Always

I tend to get anxious or worried easily.

1) Never
2) Rarely

3) Occasionally
4) Often
5) Always

I am generally aware of my emotions and can identify them accurately.

1) Never
2) Rarely
3) Occasionally
4) Often
5) Always

I am connected with my feelings and can express them freely and honestly.

1) Never
2) Rarely
3) Occasionally
4) Often
5) Always

I notice physical sensations associated with my emotions (like sweating when nervous, etc).

1) Never
2) Rarely
3) Occasionally
4) Often
5) Always

I am aware of how my emotions affect my thoughts and behaviors.

1) Never
2) Rarely
3) Occasionally
4) Often
5) Always

I often engage in healthy coping mechanisms (like exercise, meditation, and talking to a friend) whenever I am stressed or upset.

1) Never
2) Rarely
3) Occasionally
4) Often
5) Always

I resort to unhealthy coping mechanisms (like excessive drinking, emotional eating, etc.) during emotional distress.

1) Never
2) Rarely
3) Occasionally
4) Often
5) Always

I often seek support from friends or family when I am feeling down.

1) Never
2) Rarely
3) Occasionally
4) Often
5) Always

I isolate myself from others when I am feeling emotionally overwhelmed.

1) Never
2) Rarely
3) Occasionally
4) Often
5) Always

Use the following scale for your score :

Never = 1 point
Rarely = 2 points
Occasionally = 3 points
Often = 4 points
Always = 5 points

Now, according to your responses, add all the points. If your total score is:

12-30:
You have a good understanding of your emotions and you are already employing healthy coping mechanisms.

31-45:
You have a moderate level of emotional awareness and you need to work on certain areas to improve your understanding.

46-60:
There is a significant opportunity for growth to improve your emotional patterns. It is beneficial to employ various techniques to develop a better understanding of your emotions.

1. Identify Your Emotions

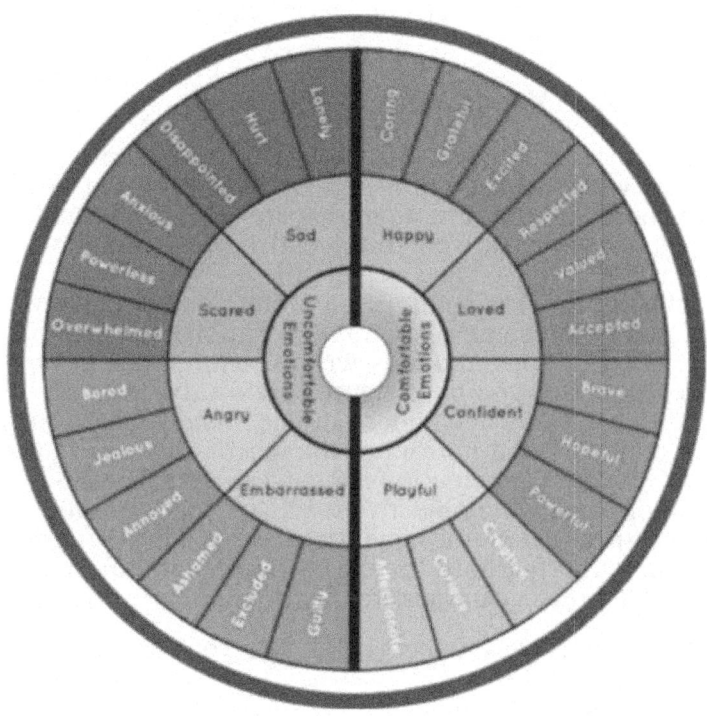

The diagram presented here is known as the "Wheel of Emotions." It is used to identify the range of different emotions we feel in a particular situation. The emotions in the inner circle are the primary emotions, which are then further divided into secondary emotions. Most of us are familiar with the ones mentioned in the inner circle, but the secondary ones are difficult to understand. However, we feel all of them at different times and we should be able to identify them before pulling the balancing act.

Think of a situation you recently experienced and select the primary and secondary emotions from the wheel. Write them down in your journal and describe their corresponding situation. Try to be as specific as possible. The results of this activity will give you a general scale of emotions you go through in a situation. It also helps you track the core reasons triggering an emotion. For instance, if you feel anxious in a situation, it probably means that you are feeling scared, so you need to fight your fears in order to deal with your anxiety.

2. Accept And Validate Your Emotions

You cannot create a healthy emotional response if you keep rejecting your own emotions. As we have seen in the wheel above, there are some emotions that are comfortable and some that are not. Usually, we like to validate those emotions that make us feel at peace and neglect the ones that make us feel uncomfortable. This habit, often unnoticed, can disrupt our emotional balance and mess up our relationships with others. So, to accept all your emotions, write a compassionate response to each emotion you have figured out in the previous step. Imagine what a kind and understanding friend might say to you. You can either stand in front of the mirror and look into your eyes to validate your emotions or you can write them down on a piece of paper. The objective is to have a conversation with yourself, speaking in the same way you would to a friend. For instance, if you felt hurt, lonely, or disappointed because you were sad, then you can validate those emotions by saying:

Emotion 1: "It is okay to feel HURT. Everyone experiences this emotion sometimes."

Emotion 2: "Feeling SAD is a natural part of being human."

Emotion 3: "I acknowledge the feeling of DISAPPOINTMENT. It is a valid response to the situation I experienced."

By writing them down in this way or saying them out loud, you practice emotional affirmations, which is the key to acceptance.

3. ABC Model

Albert Ellis's ABC Model is a valuable aspect of Rational-Emotive Behavior Therapy (REBT), a part of cognitive-behavioral therapy (CBT). The ABC Model is built on a fundamental idea – external events, represented by 'A,' do not directly cause our emotions, represented by 'C.' Instead, it is our beliefs, captured by 'B,' that comes in between and shape how we feel.

Now, here is where it gets interesting. You can use this model not just for major life events but also in your everyday, 'normal' situations. It is a tool for reflection, helping you understand why you react the way you do to various events, which, in turn, can help you respond more effectively next time.

Imagine your partner forgets to wish you a happy anniversary. Now the antecedent (A) would be your partner forgetting your anniversary. In such a situation, your behavior (B) decides the consequence (C). Instead of expressing immediate frustration, you calmly communicate your feelings with your partner. In this way, your partner will have a clear understanding of what made you upset and about your level of frustration. They would then be able to make necessary amends to make you feel better whether it is through an apology, a surprise dinner reservation, or any token of love. Through this exercise, both partners get the necessary time to think before reacting, and that fosters a climate of good communication and heightened awareness within the relationship.

4. Feedback From Others

Another healthy way to assess your emotional response is to get feedback from your partner and others who are close to you. Feedback can be a powerful tool if you look at it with a positive mindset. Often, it is the people around us who can see our emotional patterns from a different perspective and their feedback can give a clear picture of our reactions. I'm an introvert and when it comes to expressing emotions, I find it challenging. A few years back, whenever I encountered an argument with my partner, I would resort to isolation instead of addressing the conflict. This would only make the situation worse. However, once I understood the fact that I needed to improve my communication, I asked my partner what I should improve in my communication style. He gently pointed out every detail, which helped me a great deal while working on my own emotional intelligence.

5. Regularly Self-Assess Your Emotions

Things get out of control when we leave our emotions unchecked. Situations evolve and so do our emotions. We cannot feel the same way all the time; sometimes, we adopt or pick up unhealthy emotional patterns that might affect our relationships with others. So, it is wise to periodically check on our emotions. Set a specific time during the week to think about your reactions and then reflect on them to come up with better-coping mechanisms. When you constantly assess your emotions, you start understanding your triggers and then you can actively deal with them to keep the situation in your control.

Identifying Your Triggers and Responses

Dealing with our emotions can sometimes feel like trying to keep them neatly locked away in a box until we are ready to handle them, but it doesn't quite work that way. Emotions are complex and can show up at any time, whether we are prepared for them or not. Our emotions work like a built-in alarm system, giving us valuable information about what's going on inside and around us. When we understand why we are feeling a certain way, it is easier to manage and make sense of those emotions.

However, there are moments when our emotional reactions seem out of proportion to the situation. Mental health professionals call these moments "triggers," and they can be quite uncomfortable. Triggers have a way of showing up when we least expect them. So, how do we deal with triggers? How do we even identify them when they happen? Understanding how triggers form and recognizing what they feel like is the first step in coming up with a strategy to cope with them.

To protect us from future harm, our brain links the fight-or-flight response to reminders of the trauma, like specific smells, sights, or sounds. When exposed to these triggers, our bodies react as if we are in immediate danger, similar to how someone with post-traumatic stress disorder (PTSD) might feel.

Trigger symptoms can vary from person to person but often include feeling scared, anxious, or unsafe. You might experience a racing heart, sweaty palms, and difficulty breathing. At times, it can feel like your emotions are in control, leaving you feeling like you want to escape or avoid the situation entirely. Negative thoughts, mood swings, and even physical tension can all come into play. Here are a couple of ways that can help you identify when you might be triggered:

1. Notice How You Feel

Pay attention to your emotional state. Are you feeling anxious, overwhelmed, or finding it difficult to calm down? Take note of these symptoms, especially if they seem to appear suddenly and do not quite align with your current situation. If you are experiencing these intense emotions without a clear reason, it is likely a trigger is at play.

2. What Is Bothering You?

Is there something that has unexpectedly started weighing on your mind? When it comes to high-stakes or significant concerns, it is normal to feel stressed. However, if you find yourself feeling stressed or anxious over something that is usually routine or minor, there might be more to it than meets the eye.

When you are upset, it often manifests as a physical sensation in your stomach, chest, or neck. Your mind might go blank, or you could experience various symptoms as we discussed earlier. Over time, you will notice that these sensations often feel similar when you are triggered. This familiarity is a key to identifying a trigger. Once you have honed in on that feeling, you are on your way to recognizing it as a trigger. This awareness is the first step towards moving from "reaction mode" to self-care. It is essential not to react immediately when you are feeling triggered. Give yourself some space from the situation to process your emotional response. As you become more practiced at recognizing your triggers, you can develop coping mechanisms to deal with them.

Managing Impulsive Reactions

Consider impulsivity as a habit that has taken root over the years. It is something you do almost automatically, without much thought. Whether it is making impulsive decisions about relationships or spending, it can lead to consequences that may not be in your best interest in the long run.

1. Take a Pause

When you feel that impulsivity is creeping in, take a deep breath and pause. Give yourself some time before you decide to go ahead with it. Now, here is why this pause is essential! In the heat of the moment, impulsive decisions might seem like a quick fix for your feelings. Maybe going shopping or buying that fancy new video game feels like it is going to bring you instant gratification. But here's the catch – that immediate satisfaction often fades away faster than you'd expect.

It's more important to consider the long-term consequences. Ask yourself, "Will this impulsive action bring more harm or benefit down the road?" The truth is, while the thrill of the moment may be short-lived, the repercussions can linger. That new video game? It might be fun for a while, but the financial strain it causes could last longer. It could jeopardize a meaningful relationship you have built.

2. Remove or Avoid Your Triggers

Impulsive reactions are often triggered by certain actions or situations. And keeping those triggers out of the equation can help prevent the impulse reactions. Let me paint a vivid picture here to address one of the most common triggers that couples experience. You and your partner are on a romantic gateway. You both are enjoying the most scenic mountain view ever while cherishing the time you are spending together. Suddenly, you receive a work email, and you start looking at the phone screen for the next hour. Now, this may trigger your partner to act upset. Out of impulse, they might decide to return home. In situations like these, keeping your phone away for a while would work.

Even if you have to balance work with personal life on a holiday, designate a separate time to read and respond to your work emails. This makes sure that when you promise to spend your time with your partner, you stay free of distractions.

3. Find a Constructive Outlet

If you are someone who enjoys a good adrenaline rush and often resorts to impulsive actions to satisfy that thrill-seeking craving, there are better alternatives. It is all about finding a hobby or activity that can be a fulfilling outlet for your need for excitement, minus the impulsiveness. Instead of impulsively acting on your thrill-seeking or endorphin-boosting instincts, you might want to consider some activities that give you that same heart-pounding, exhilarating feeling but in a more structured and controlled way.

One option could be taking up a kickboxing class or another form of physical activity or exercise. It is a fantastic way to release pent-up energy and experience the thrill of physical activity in a structured and organized environment. You will get to challenge yourself, push your limits and, at the same time, keep your impulsive tendencies in check.

By going for these activities, you are not only satisfying your thrill-seeking side in a healthier manner but also ensuring that your impulsive behaviors do not harm your relationships. It is all about balancing your need for excitement with a structured approach.

Calming The Storm Within

Stress, it can get to the best of us, right? It is our body's ancient "fight or flight" mode kicking in, ready to protect us from danger. It is the brain's way of saying, "Get ready to make some quick decisions!" So, what happens next? Your heart starts pounding, flooding your muscles with blood, your breathing goes into overdrive, and that adrenaline? It is a shot of energy. In today's fast-paced world, all these physical reactions can kick in not just during life-threatening situations, but also because of mundane stressors like rush-hour traffic, a hectic workday or even catching up on the latest news.

Now, we might not have a magic wand to zap away daily stress entirely, but we do have some tricks up our sleeves to help you recalibrate. So, what do you say we dive into a few handy strategies?

1. Grounding Technique - To Reset Your Mind

The Grounding Chair exercise is a wonderful way to quickly calm yourself and develop self-awareness. It is a mini mindfulness journey that connects you with the present moment. For this exercise, find a comfy chair and settle into it. Close your eyes and take a deep breath. Now count to three as you breathe in and out, a simple rhythm to help you focus. Then, shift your attention to your body. Feel how it sits in the chair, how your legs and feet make contact with the ground. Pay attention to the texture of the fabric beneath you, the sensation of the seat against your body.

Here comes the grounding part. Visualize your feet pushing down as if they are connecting with the Earth. Picture your energy flowing from your head, down through your body, and out through your feet into the Earth.

As this energy flows down from your head, notice how every part of your body starts to feel heavier and more relaxed. It is a gentle release of tension. Feel this sense of heaviness moving down your legs, through your feet, and into the ground.

This exercise is like a reset button for your mind and body. It is a way to bring yourself back to the present moment, grounding you in the here and now. It can be incredibly calming and is a powerful tool for building self-awareness.

2. Paced Breathing

'Paced Breathing' might sound a bit cliché, but trust me, it is one of the best ways to help manage those emotions. You are going to focus on your exhale, making it a tad longer than your inhale. And guess what? This little tweak also works its magic on our parasympathetic nervous system, helping us find that extra dose of calm. To give it a whirl, just count how long your inhale is in your head and as you exhale, make sure you are counting at the same pace, but aim for it to be at least a smidge longer than your inhale. For instance, if you reach a count of 4 when you inhale, make sure your exhale lasts at least 5.

3. Step Back

When you are feeling stressed out, it can often feel like the end of the world, right? Here is a little trick to help you calm those nerves. Take a step back and try to see the bigger picture. Think about how the stressful situation fits into your entire life, your grand scheme of things. This simple exercise helps you view your stress from a more objective angle. You might just realize that the thing causing you all this stress isn't as catastrophic as it seems. Step back to get a better perspective on the situation as that can be really helpful in making the stress feel more manageable.

4. The Forward Bend

For this exercise, bend over and touch your toes, and if you cannot quite reach them, no worries, no flexibility judgment here! You can even do this while sitting, just stick your head between your knees. Take some slow, deep breaths while you hang out in that forward bend position for about 30 to 60 seconds if you can. What's cool is that this forward bend move activates our parasympathetic nervous system - you know, the "rest and digest" system. That would be like flipping the switch to slow down and feel a bit calmer. When you are ready to stand up again, do not rush it; you do not want any falling-over mishaps.

5. Reduce The Intensity by Acting The Opposite

The big question is, do you want to dial down that emotion's intensity? You see, emotions show up for a reason; they have their own story to tell, and it is crucial to listen closely to what they are trying to convey. But there are moments when emotions spill their message and then refuse to leave the stage, causing all sorts of trouble. Take anger, for example. Imagine you have had a heated argument with your partner, and you want to have a productive conversation to resolve things, but the anger is still swirling around you, making it nearly impossible to have that talk. That is the perfect time to consider dialing down the anger's intensity. Anxiety is another good example. Say you are anxious about being in a social gathering, even though you logically know there is no real threat to your safety. This anxiety is cramping your style and preventing you from enjoying social activities. It is in moments like these when we can experiment with acting oppositely to the emotion.

If you are dealing with anger, the opposite action might entail gently creating some space between you and the person you are mad at. For instance, they are in the living room watching TV and you decide to go into your bedroom to read for a while. Alternatively, it might mean treating the person civilly and respectfully, focusing on not making things worse, and maintaining a decent attitude. But if you retreat to the bedroom and keep stewing over the situation or thinking judgmental thoughts about the other person, your anger will just keep on simmering. In this case, it is not just about acting opposite to your actions; you might need to give it a try with your thoughts too. Perhaps shift your focus to the positive qualities of the person or the things you appreciate about them.

6. Find Your Flow

Have you experienced those moments when you are really focused and everything just clicks? Like you are in the zone. Well, we call that finding your "flow." You do not have to be running a marathon or doing something physical to get in the flow. You can use the same techniques to stay productive and block out all those pesky distractions, especially when you are feeling stressed. It is your secret weapon for getting stuff done and keeping that stress at bay!

7. Cognitive Restructuring

"What if I mess this up?"... "What if I am not good enough?" Negative thoughts like those often hit our minds and trigger our emotions in a way that would disrupt an otherwise normal situation. It is fine and completely natural to have such thoughts. It is our mind's natural mechanism to protect itself by being cautious. People who have experienced more emotional damage frequently get these thoughts. If you go through the same, then restructuring your mindset can help you a great deal. Instead of letting those negative thoughts amplify intense emotions, you can balance them with counter-positive thoughts and manage your emotions accordingly. You can do this by employing positive affirmations. If your mind tells you that you are going to mess this up, tell yourself that:

I am strong and capable of handling every situation.

Or

I am in control of my thoughts and choose to focus on what I can change. I release what I cannot control.

This opens your mind to new ideas and boosts your self-esteem and eventually, you will start seeing yourself as a confident person. To practice this exercise, stand in front of a mirror, look yourself in the eyes, and repeat the affirmations out loud 3-5 times at a minimum. This process encourages you to think rationally and helps to reduce the impact of negative emotions.

How Do Affirmations Work?

Just as receiving compliments or words of appreciation from others boosts your confidence, receiving the same self-affirming words from yourself significantly increases your self-esteem. The effects of positive affirmations on self-esteem are also supported by several scientific studies. In a research study conducted in 2016, researchers found that telling yourself affirming words like "I am strong, I am confident, or I am capable" activates the reward system in the brain. When the reward system is triggered, it helps alleviate stress and gives you the strength to overcome any pain or struggle. Positive affirmations also help you cope with uncertainty and enable you to take targeted actions.

Exercise: Affirmations

This is quite simple and easy to practice. You just have to sit alone without distraction. Either look yourself in the mirror (which is preferable) or just imagine that you are talking to yourself face-to-face and then for the next 3-5 minutes say 5-10 positive self-affirming sentences. Such as:

I am worthy of love and kindness. I embrace the power within me to create the life I desire.

Every challenge I face is an opportunity to grow and improve.

I am confident, capable, and resilient.

I trust in my ability to make the right decisions for myself.

I am deserving of success and will achieve my goals.

I radiate positivity, and it attracts positivity into my life.

I am in control of my thoughts and choose to focus on the good.

I am surrounded by love and support.

My past does not define me; I create my own path and my own happiness.

Now, you can pick and choose the affirmations that resonate with you. Regular practice of this exercise can miraculously boost your confidence.

Chapter 3

IGNITING PASSION FROM WITHIN

For Relationship Success

"Passion is energy. Feel the power that comes from focusing on what excites you." - Oprah Winfrey

In my relationship, my partner and I unearthed the profound impact of kindling passion from within. We both are fervent lovers of nature, so we make time to go hiking and explore the great outdoors. Rather than allowing our relationship to plateau into predictability, we made it a ritual to go on spontaneous hiking adventures to various trails and mountains. Our shared love for nature became the driving force behind our enduring connection and sense of thrill. Our mutual love for hiking not only ignited our curiosity but also inspired us to tackle challenges together, fostering a perpetual sense of wonder and mutual growth. Through our shared passion, we discovered not only immediate excitement but also a lasting, deep-rooted bond that strengthened our relationship.

True passion isn't just a fleeting emotion; it is an intrinsic flame that resides within us and drives us to connect with our partners. When both partners nurture a passion for life, it breathes vitality into the relationship. Your passion inspires creativity, nurtures shared interests, and fuels a continuous journey of learning and growth together. It fills your moments with excitement and opens the door to explore the world and each other with open hearts.

Passion Within

To ignite passion in your relationship, you must carry the flames of passion within yourself. There must be something that kindles your interests and creativity and keeps you motivated. So, as we dive into this chapter, we will explore how to ignite that inner passion and let it be the driving force behind a thriving and fulfilling relationship.

1. What Is Your Big Picture Plan?

It is your way of saying, *"This is where I want to go,"* or *"This is where we want to take our relationship."* Think of it as a compass. You know, the kind of explorers used to find their way in uncharted territory. Your future plan serves as your very own compass in life. It is there to help you navigate, especially when you face important decisions.

Let's say one of the aspects of your relationship vision is to foster continuous growth and support for each other's personal development. Now, when you encounter decisions as a couple, you can refer to your shared compass and ask, *"Does this choice contribute to our mutual goal of supporting each other's growth?"* This plan becomes a guiding force, helping you both align your actions with your collective vision for a thriving and supportive partnership.

2. Discover Your Core Values

Your values offer inspiration and motivation. They are the emotional drivers behind your actions. When your personal vision is aligned with your values, it acts as a constant source of motivation. Your passion is fueled by your commitment to what you truly care about. Your core values help you prioritize. When you know what's most important to you, it becomes easier to set goals and create a vision plan that revolves around those values. Your passion often emerges from the things you value the most. If you and your partner share similar values, then you can both use them as a source of inspiration to strengthen your bond. If one of your core values is "creativity," then as a couple you can dedicate time to creative activities or launch a creative business.

Your passion for creativity is right there, reflecting your values.

3. Practice Passion Mapping

Passion mapping is a technique to create a colorful roadmap to your inner fire, your passions, and what truly makes your heart sing. Consider it as an exciting journey of self-discovery that helps you explore and understand your deepest interests, desires, and dreams. You can create a passion map with your partner to identify your passions individually and then mark the ones that are common.

Take a big, blank sheet of paper and place it like a canvas in front of you. Now, use this canvas as a visual representation of your passions and fill it with all the things that ignite your enthusiasm. Divide the sheet into three portions, one for you, one for your partner, and the middle one for the passions you both share. Now, you both need to start by asking yourself some key questions:

- What activities make you lose track of time?

- What are you curious about?

- What gives you a sense of purpose or fulfillment?

These questions are your tools to uncover your passions.

Let's say one of your answers is *"travel."* You have always loved exploring new places, learning about different cultures, and meeting people from all walks of life. Travel is a passion of yours and you add it to your canvas. Now, you move on to the next question: *"What skills or talents do I have?"* Maybe you are a gifted musician and playing an instrument brings you immense joy. That goes on your canvas too.

You and your partner can continue this process, adding more and more elements to your individual passion map. Once your respective canvas is filled, you step back and take a look. Now see the visual representation of your inner world, your unique combination of passions. This map serves as a reminder of what makes you feel alive and what you want to pursue in life. Compare your passion maps and pick out the activities which you both are passionate about then place them in the middle portion. Now you both know the convergence points of your relationship and you can carry out the activities to strengthen your bond.

And here is the beauty of passion mapping, it doesn't have to be static. Your passions can evolve, and your map can change over time as you explore new interests and uncover more about yourself. It is a tool for self-discovery, motivation, and a reminder of what truly sets your soul on fire. So, grab your canvas and start mapping your passions – it is a journey that leads to a more vibrant and fulfilling life.

4. Discover Your Hobbies

Tuning into your hobbies is like pressing the "passion" button in your life. It is a way to reconnect with what makes your heart dance. Hobbies not only let you connect with your inner self, but they also have this magical way of transforming your relationship with your partner. Discovering shared hobbies with your partner can be a great way to spend time doing something that you both enjoy and ignite passion in your relationship. Let's assume that you and your partner have a shared interest in music. You love to play piano, and your partner loves to play guitar. Both of you can jam to your favorite songs together! Now, music becomes the magnet that pulls you closer together. This can be true for any other hobby or activity, be it gardening, crafting, cooking, playing sports, gaming, hiking, climbing, etc. The catch is to find activities that you both find pleasure in.

Dedicate time for exploration. Schedule regular "passion time" with your partner It might be a few hours a week or a day dedicated to trying something new. This time allows you to get into different hobbies without distractions.

5. Things You Do Not Like

It is natural to focus on the things we love and enjoy in life. After all, those are the moments that make our hearts sing. But there is also a special kind of wisdom in taking a closer look at the things we do not love.

For instance, imagine you and your partner occasionally engage in activities that leave you both feeling a bit unfulfilled or uninspired. It could be a routine date night that doesn't spark excitement or a certain topic of conversation that feels draining. Taking a closer look at these aspects allows you to understand more about each other's preferences and needs.

As you assess what doesn't bring joy, you might discover that spontaneity and more diverse conversation topics are what you both crave. This realization becomes a key to unlocking a deeper connection. It helps you understand that you both thrive when there's variety and room for creative expression in your relationship.

So, when you assess activities you do not love, you are essentially peeling back the layers to reveal your authentic self. It is a valuable process because it guides you towards making choices that are more in line with your passions and values.

6. Release Limiting Beliefs

It is often our self-limiting beliefs that stop us from doing what we really want to do. While releasing such beliefs as individuals is crucial, it is also important to do the same as a couple. Choose a calm and quiet place where you won't be disturbed. Sit or lie down in a comfortable position. You can close your eyes or leave them open, depending on your preference. Pay attention to your thoughts without judgment. When limiting beliefs arise, do not push them away or criticize yourself. Simply observe them. When you notice a limiting belief, acknowledge it. Say something like, "I see this thought, but it doesn't define me." Then, gently let it go, like a leaf floating away on a stream.

Take deep, calming breaths as you release these thoughts. With each exhale, imagine yourself letting go of these beliefs. After releasing limiting beliefs, reframe them with positive and empowering thoughts. For example, if you have let go of the belief that you are not creative, replace it with, "I am capable of expressing my creativity in unique ways."

7. Cultivate Gratitude

Dedicate a few minutes each day to write down aspects of your passions for which you are grateful. Be specific in your gratitude. Instead of saying, "*I'm grateful for my passion for art,*" say something like, "*I'm grateful for the feeling of pure joy I get when I'm painting.*" As you write, reflect on how your passions have enriched your life and brought you happiness. This deepens your appreciation.

8. Set Intention

Clearly define how you want to integrate your passion into your life. What specific actions can you take? Develop a practical plan with achievable steps. For instance, if your passion is writing, set a daily writing goal or decide to attend a writing workshop. Put your plan into your schedule. Block out time for your passion, treating it as a non-negotiable commitment. Regularly review your progress and adjust your plan as needed. Mindfulness can help you stay focused on your intention.

9. Visualize Your Goals

You know, there is something magical about the power of visualization. It helps you paint a vivid picture in your mind of what you want to achieve, and it can be a game-changer when it comes to igniting your inner passion.

Visualizing your goals is like creating a mental movie of your desired future. When you close your eyes and imagine yourself living your dream, it does something incredible to your brain and your heart. It becomes a source of inspiration, like a guiding light that helps you stay on track and excited about your journey.

Let me give you an example. Think of an aspiring artist who dreams of having their own art gallery one day. They are deeply passionate about painting, but the road to owning a gallery can be challenging. There are days when self-doubt creeps in. That is where visualization comes in.

Every morning, this artist takes a few minutes to sit quietly and visualize their gallery. They imagine the vibrant colors on the walls, the excited chatter of visitors, and the feeling of accomplishment that washes over them. They picture themselves creating new artwork and seeing it proudly displayed.

This daily practice stirs up their passion. It reminds them why they started this journey in the first place. It keeps their goals at the forefront of their mind, even on the toughest days when they feel like giving up.

10. Break Free From the Pressure Chains

External validation and societal expectations can be like heavy chains that weigh down our passions. They can keep us from truly pursuing what lights up our souls. Imagine these expectations as a crowd of people constantly whispering, "Are you sure you are doing the right thing?"

But when you decide to release that grip on external validation, it lets you reclaim your personal power. It is about saying, "I'm doing this for me because it is what I love, not just to win approval from others."

For instance, think of someone who's passionate about art. They might have hesitated to pursue it as a career because they were told that a 'stable job' in a different field was a safer choice. But the moment they decide to embrace their love for art and create, they are setting themselves free from that external pressure. They are choosing their passion over societal expectations.

Igniting Passion in One Another

Your emotional intelligence plays a pivotal role in fostering connection and intimacy with your partner. I have seen several couples losing their spark over the years and blaming one another for not investing enough into the relationship. The major problem is that it takes consistent efforts and constant input to keep that same passion ignited. The kind of dedication required for that comes from discovering passion within. When you discover yourself, unlock newer levels of self-awareness, and become more in tune with your own emotions, only then you become able to make the right moves and spark a similar passion in your partner. While the activities and techniques shared in the previous section can help you kindle your inner passion, the following techniques will help you and your partner align your values and keep your passion for one another ignited.

1. Go the Extra Mile Every Now and Then

Remember those times at the start of your relationship when you'd go the extra mile to make your partner feel extra special? Well, why not bring back those efforts? It's a sweet surprise that will show your partner just how much you still love them. You don't have to do it every day, but a little "above and beyond" every now and then never hurt anyone! For example, you can remember your partner's favorite childhood snack, search high and low to find it, and surprise them with a stash of those nostalgic treats on a random Tuesday, just because you know it will make them smile.

2. Express Your Gratitude

Ever catch yourself feeling really grateful when your partner does something thoughtful for you? Well, make sure to let them know! It is all about better communication and positive vibes. A simple *"Thank you for..."* can go a long way in letting your partner know you appreciate them. For instance, your partner spends the entire weekend tackling household chores that you both dread. Instead of taking it for granted, you look them in the eyes and say, "Thank you for taking care of all that. I really appreciate it. You make our home a better place."

3. Sprinkle a Little Consideration

Your partner might be the one person you can be totally up front with but don't forget to sprinkle in some consideration. Venting is cool, but being considerate is even cooler. Keep it in mind when you are chilling with your partner. Let's say, you had a rough day at work, and you are venting to your partner. Instead of continuing to watch their favorite show, they put it on pause, look at you, and say, *"I'm here for you. Let's talk about it. What can I do to support you right now?"*

4. Plan Your Date Nights

Life gets crazy busy, but don't forget to carve out some alone time with your partner. Date nights and trying out new things together are still a must, even if your schedules are packed. For example, despite both of you having busy schedules, you take the initiative to plan a surprise date night. You arrange for a cozy picnic under the stars in your backyard, complete with fairy lights and their favorite snacks.

5. Enjoy Your Time Together

Affection isn't just about what happens in the bedroom. Start with sweet touches and hugs. Then, cozy up on the couch together – just enjoy being close. It is the little things that count. Instead of just sitting side by side on the couch watching TV, you turn off the screens, cuddle up, and share stories about your day. The focus is on each other, with occasional laughter and shared moments that strengthen your connection.

6. Be Adventurous Together

Adventure time! What is your idea of an adventure? Discuss your dream adventures with your partner and look out for activities that you can enjoy doing together. Exciting activities have a magical way of sparking passion. For instance, you and your partner can decide to try something completely out of your comfort zone, like taking a spontaneous dance class. The laughter, the awkward moves, and the shared experience create a lasting memory and bring a new level of excitement to your relationship.

7. Have Some Alone Time

Everyone needs a breather. Spend some time apart from your partner – it is healthy. Plus, it builds up anticipation for the things you have planned together. You recognize that your partner needs a bit of solo time to recharge, so you encourage them to take an afternoon for themselves. It could be reading a book, going for a walk, or simply having some quiet time to relax.

8. Communicate More

Keep the conversation flowing about your dreams and goals. Plans may not always go as expected, but chatting about where you see things going can be just as thrilling as reminiscing about the early days of your relationship. You set aside dedicated time each week for a "dreams and goals" conversation with your partner. You discuss your individual aspirations and how you can support each other in achieving them, creating a shared vision for the future.

9. Surprise!

Time for a surprise! Treat your partner to a thoughtful gift. It doesn't have to break the bank – you could even make it yourself. The key is to show them that you care, and a little surprise does the trick nicely. You notice your partner eyeing a vintage record player in a shop window, but they haven't bought it. Later, you surprise them by bringing it home, saying, "*I saw you admiring it and I thought it would be a great addition to our home. Happy surprise day!*"

PART II

Building Deep Connections with Your Partner Through Emotional Intelligence Mastery

Chapter 4
EMPATHY
The Secret Ingredient to a Stronger Bond

"When someone really hears you without passing judgment on you, without trying to take responsibility for you, without trying to mold you, it feels damn good." - Carl Rogers

Empathy is the cornerstone of a deep and meaningful relationship. It is indeed the secret sauce that strengthens the bond between two partners. Whether it is a disagreement or a conflict, having empathy for another lets you reach a positive solution to de-escalate the situation. When you practice empathy, you create a safe haven for you and your partner where feelings can be expressed openly, and together, you both foster trust, intimacy, and acceptance. Empathy allows you to step into each other's shoes while offering unwavering support and validation. In moments of joy, it intensifies the closeness and during times of sorrow, it offers comfort. Through empathy, you can navigate challenges with understanding, compassion, and enduring love.

What Does It Mean to Be Empathic?

Being empathic means having the ability to understand and share the feelings of your partner. It gives you the capacity to put yourself in your partner's shoes, to understand their emotions, and to respond with the kind of sensitivity and compassion required in the situation. Empathy goes beyond sympathy, as it calls for a deeper emotional connection and an active effort to grasp and resonate with the emotions of others.

Imagine your partner has had a rough day at work. They come home feeling stressed and frustrated. Instead of dismissing their feelings or offering immediate solutions, you respond empathically. You might say, *"I can see that today was really tough for you. It sounds like you are feeling overwhelmed. I am here for you. How can I support you right now?"* This response shows understanding and a willingness to share in your partner's emotions.

Our emotional intelligence and the compassion we have for our partner come into play here. It is not just understanding their pain on a surface level; it is a deep, heartfelt connection because we can put ourselves in their shoes. This kind of empathy strengthens our bond with our partner and shows that we are there to support them through difficult times. It is a testament to the depth of our relationship and our emotional connection.

It indicates that we are in the same emotional boat, navigating those rough waters together, which can bring us closer and strengthen our relationship. Emotional empathy is all about sharing similar emotional experiences. It is having a strong emotional connection because you have been through comparable situations or emotions.

Understanding Your Partner's Perspective

"Empathy is patiently and sincerely seeing the world from the other person's perspective of view." - Albert Einstein

When it comes to relationships, conflicts often arise from the inability to understand our partner's perspective. It is the failure to truly comprehend where they are coming from and that leads to disagreement, misunderstandings, and discord. Empathy in such situations, acts as a powerful lens that gives us the ability to see through our partner's eyes, look into their emotions, and understand the thoughts and motives behind their actions. When we embrace empathy, we develop the capacity to navigate our partner's mind. It lets us acknowledge their feelings, validate their experiences, and create a genuine connection based on understanding.

It is easier said than done! When you are in a heated argument with your partner, it is difficult to keep your mind straight and put yourself in your partner's shoes. Having said that, I believe there are various strategies that we can consciously employ to allow ourselves to comprehend other's perspectives.

1. Ask For What They Want

In any relationship, it is essential to approach your partner's perspective with openness and empathy. Instead of dismissing their point of view and potentially hurting their feelings, try to help them ease out of any distress they may be experiencing. Do not view differing opinions as a source of conflict; consider them opportunities to gain deeper insights into your partner. Instead of assuming and second-guessing anything, it is best to simply ask your partner about their thoughts. You can ask your partner these simple questions to gain insights and understand them better. Remember that in moments of high emotion, your vocal tone and pitch should be sympathetic, quiet, and low. To ask the following questions in a voice high with tension would be counter-productive and not indicative of feelings of empathy with their perspective:

- *"What are you seeing that I am not?"*

This question invites your partner to share their unique perspective and sheds light on aspects you might not have considered. It encourages open dialogue and allows you to see things from their point of view.

- *"What have you experienced in your past that has led you to this belief?"*

It is imperative to understand your partner's past experiences and how they shape their current beliefs in building a stronger connection. This question helps you appreciate the context behind their opinions and emotions.

- *"How can I use this as an opportunity to understand you better?"*

Acknowledge your partner's viewpoint as a chance to deepen your understanding of who they are. When you ask this question, you convey your genuine interest in them and their feelings, making them feel valued and secure.

When you approach your partner's perspective with receptivity, it not only eases any tension but also changes the overall energy of the relationship. Your partner will feel truly understood, which enhances their sense of safety and security. This newfound security will encourage them to open up more and share because they trust that you won't use their vulnerability against them.

2. Listen With Curiosity Instead of Judgment

Start listening to your partner like they are telling you a story about someone else, even if it is about you. Get curious about how they are feeling here, why they think the way they do, and what impact this has on them. Ask powerful, curious questions to encourage your partner to share more about what they are thinking, feeling, and experiencing so you can deepen your understanding of them. Resist your urge to react or fight back. You cannot understand if you are thinking about what you are going to say next!

3. Understand Before Trying to Be Understood

When we communicate with a partner, we are often trying to highlight our point of view and make sure we are heard and understood. But when we show empathetic concern and try to understand our partner and where they are coming from, we can assess and offer a positive response to the problem instead of escalating it. The empathetic concern goes beyond mere sympathy or understanding. It means that you genuinely feel your partner's joy, sadness, or any other emotion. You are not just an observer; you are emotionally invested in their well-being. Here is how you can show empathetic concern towards your partner:

- *Comfort during tough times:* When your partner is going through a difficult period, you not only understand their pain but also genuinely care about making them feel better. You offer emotional support, a listening ear, or a shoulder to lean on because you deeply empathize with their distress.

- *Celebrating their successes:* In times of happiness and success, you share in your partner's joy and excitement. You do not just acknowledge their achievements; you are genuinely thrilled for them, and their happiness brings you happiness as well.

- *Being attuned to their needs:* You are emotionally tuned in to your partner's needs, sometimes even before they express them. For example, you may sense when they have had a tiring day and offer to take care of certain responsibilities to make their evening more relaxing.

- *Conflict resolution:* When conflicts arise, you approach them with empathy and concern. You are not focused on winning an argument but on understanding your partner's perspective and finding solutions that are mutually satisfying.

4. Respect The Differences

No two people can completely agree on every single subject. Difference of opinion is as natural as breathing air. So, throw away the idea that in order to be in sync with your partner you both need to have the same opinion on everything. You just need to learn how to agree to disagree while respecting each other's differences. This realization comes naturally when you start seeing yourself in your partner's shoes and recognizing the reasons behind their beliefs and actions.

5. Imago Dialogue

This technique was presented by Dr. Harville Hendrix. It is mainly a structured communication method that helps to create empathetic understanding between partners.

It has three essential steps:

- the first is Mirroring,

- the second is Validating, and

- the third is Empathizing.

During the Mirroring step, one partner shares while the other listens without interruption. The listener then paraphrases what they have heard without analyzing or modifying the content, making sure to have an accurate understanding. In the Validating step, the listener confirms the logical sense of their partner's message and asks for clarification if needed. Finally, in the last step, Empathizing, the listener guesses their partner's feelings based on the expressed thoughts while giving an emotional dimension to the conversation.

Now the question arises, how can you employ this technique? Well, it is best to share this technique with your partner so that you both can use it to understand each other better. But if you want to employ it first before asking your partner to do the same, here is how you can do it:

Let's say you are having a disagreement about spending habits with your partner. How can you employ the Imago dialogue here? Let me explain!

The first step is "**Mirroring**", right? So, for that, you must listen to your partner actively and then paraphrase the things they said.

For instance, your partner says:
"I feel frustrated because I think we need to save more money, but you keep making impulsive purchases without discussing it with me."

Without reacting to the statement, clarify the cause behind it. You can paraphrase that as:
"So, you are feeling frustrated because you believe we should be saving more and my impulsive purchases without discussion upset you. Did I understand that correctly?"

Now comes the "**Validation**" step:

Now that you have listened to your partner's concerns and understood them, it's time to validate. You can say something like:
"That makes sense; I understand your concerns about our finances. Can you tell me more about the situations where my purchases bothered you?"

In response to that your partner will get the perfect window to share their true feelings about your purchases and the real reasons why they are so concerned about finances.

In return, you need to show **"Empathy"** as the final step of this technique:
"I can imagine you might be feeling anxious about our financial stability and maybe even a bit neglected. Let's discuss your concerns then and find some optimal solution together."

By practicing those three steps every time you have an argument, you give yourself and your partner the necessary time to think and respond while avoiding any misunderstanding (the root cause of most relationship problems). This exercise works best if both partners practice it, but if either one of them starts employing it, that would significantly improve mutual understanding.

6. Emotionally Focused Therapy

Another wonderful technique for better understanding your partner's perspective is Emotionally Focused Therapy, pioneered by Dr. Sue Johnson. Dr. Johnson, a compassionate clinical psychologist, emphasizes the importance of recognizing and validating our partner's emotions as a cornerstone for building emotional intimacy and deep connection in a relationship. Validation involves acknowledging and accepting your partner's feelings without any judgment or criticism. When we express genuine understanding and empathy towards our partner's emotions, we create a safe and nurturing space where they can feel heard, valued, and fully supported. This sense of security benefits both of you, fostering emotional trust and a profound sense of closeness in your relationship.

Let's assume that your partner is going through some stress about work; you can validate their feelings by saying:
"I can see that you have had a tough day at work and you are feeling really stressed about the situation. It must be really challenging for you."

This validation shows empathy, showing that you respect and value your partner's emotional experience. Your partner will in turn feel heard and supported, which will lead to a deeper emotional connection between you two.

Active Listening Techniques

These effective techniques may sound too simple to you, but

they work like magic. The simple act of listening can work like a charm when it comes to strengthening relationships. Due to our ever-busy lives, we often forget to carve time for active communication with our partners. Most of the time we listen to each other while being busy with work or chores and that is not enough. In order to create a deeper bond with our partners, we need to sit down with them every once in a while and listen to each other without any distractions. This simple activity fights miscommunication like a hero and brings empathy and understanding to the relationship. There are several different ways through which you can employ active listening:

1. Reflective Listening

This technique was proposed by Carl Rogers. To practice this technique, one partner has to mirror the feelings of the other partner. This partner has to convey that they truly comprehend what the other one is experiencing.

For instance, if your partner says to you:
"I had a really stressful day at work."

You could reply back:
"I am sorry to hear that you had such a stressful day. It must have been tough for you. I am here for you if you want to talk about it or if there's anything I can do to help you unwind."

By repeating and reflecting the same emotions as your partner experiences, you show that you listen and care.

2. Paraphrase What You Hear

Now this one is a really great exercise. Relationship expert John Gottman suggested paraphrasing as a legitimate communication strategy for enhanced understanding and validation in relationships. When you paraphrase, you summarize what your partner has said using your own words. The goal is to confirm your understanding of their message. You see, miscommunication is the biggest enemy of empathy, and practicing this exercise prevents that. Allow me to explain it with an example.

If one partner does not feel appreciated in a relationship, then he/she can say:

"I'm frustrated because I feel like you do not appreciate my efforts."

Now, the other partner has to confirm those feelings by paraphrasing what is being said:
"So, you are saying that you feel unappreciated for the things you do?"

In this scenario, when one partner communicates their frustration about not feeling appreciated, the other one engages in paraphrasing by restating Partner A's statement in their own words.

3. Ask Open-Ended Questions

Stephen R. Covey gave another amazing technique to foster empathy and that is to ask open-ended questions in conversations with your partner. A simple yes or no response might leave room for a lot of confusion, misinterpretations, and misassumptions. It is best to ask open-ended questions in every situation to give your partner room to explain their thoughts and feelings in every situation.

For example, instead of asking your partner: *"Did you have a good day?"*,
ask: *"How was your day? Anything exciting happened today?"*

Or during a conflict, instead of asking: *"So, you don't want to talk to me?"*,
ask your partner: *"Why do you not want to discuss this matter with me?"*

4. When In Doubt, Clarify

Daniel Goleman believes that clarifying is a crucial component of active listening. Without clarifying your confusion, you cannot continue having meaningful communication with your partner. If one thing does not make sense to you, then stop, reflect, and ask your partner all the necessary questions to clear your mind and only then move ahead. If you keep ignoring little miscommunications, ultimately, they will lead to bigger conflicts that are hard to resolve. So, it is better to fix the problem right in the beginning.

If you go home one day and find your partner angry or frustrated, instead of avoiding confrontation, ask your partner what is bothering them. If your partner gives you a reason like feeling burdened or tired, then ask *"What can I do to make you feel less burdened?"* The more you ask, the more you will understand how to comfort your partner.

5. Empathetic Responses

The renowned researcher, Brene Brown, is of the view that having empathy for one another is good, but what makes it effective is how you express it. An empathetic response helps you build a deeper emotional connection with your partner. When you use just the right words and express that you care through the magic of those words then it not only calms your partner down but also creates a positive atmosphere for your relationship to grow. Some good examples of such responses are:

"I hear you. That must be really challenging for you."

"I can imagine that makes you feel [____ emotion]. I'm here for you."

"I'm sorry you are feeling this way. Is there anything specific you need from me right now?"

"I understand that this situation is making you [_____ emotion]. It is okay to feel that way and I'm here with you."

"Thank you for sharing this with me. I appreciate your honesty and am here to listen and support you."

"It sounds like you are feeling [_____ emotion]. I want you to know that your feelings matter, and I care about how you are doing."

Those words emphasize your partner's importance in your life and make them feel valued. You can tailor similar responses to suit different situations. For instance, if your partner says:

"I'm really anxious about the upcoming presentation."

You can then say: *"I understand that presentations can be nerve-wracking. How can I support you?"*

6. Thich Nhat Hanh

Mindful listening is a transformative technique that was proposed by renowned Zen master Thich Nhat Hanh to enhance relationships. Being mindful is to be present in the current moment. So, whenever your partner shows the need to talk to you, you should listen to them mindfully. Instead of looking at your phone screen or doing some work, put everything aside and just listen to your partner, making eye contact. This simple technique makes both partners feel valued, respected, and heard.

If your partner says: *"I need to talk to you about something important."*

Here is what you should do! Put away your phone and give your full attention, then say, *"I'm here and ready to listen."*

7. Resisting The Urge to Interrupt

Dale Carnegie believes that interruption is the enemy of communication and respectful dialogue. If your partner is explaining something to you, it is best to let them finish and then respond to that information. When we interrupt in the middle of a conversation or an argument, we create space for confusion and disagreement which is never good for a relationship. It is wise to show patience and resist your urge to interrupt. You can do this by practicing self-control on a daily basis.

If your partner says,
"Let me finish my thought, please."

Try to listen without interruption and say,
"I'm sorry, go on."

By doing this, you show respect for yourself and establish space for healthy communication. If you let your partner share, they will be more likely to reciprocate, paving the way for deep and meaningful conversation.

Chapter 5

SOCIAL SKILLS

Your Pathway to Effective Communication

Most people equate social skills with being more talkative and expressive - but that is not the case. It is more about the art of knowing what to say, when and how to say it, and when not to say anything. With emotional intelligence comes the inherent understanding of complex situations and you learn to react according to the need of the hour. While navigating the complexities of relationships, it is imperative to develop those social skills through the lens of emotional intelligence. Social skills guide you toward effective communication and genuine connection. These skills are the compass that helps both partners in a relationship steer through the complexities of emotions and conversations while building understanding and empathy.

The Art of Non-Verbal Communication

Yes, healthy verbal communication does hold great importance when it comes to building a deeper connection with your partner. Sometimes we miss a lot of obvious cues, signs, and expressions that reveal more about a person than their expressed words. Whatever a person faces or feels initially reflects through obvious facial expressions, as well as more subtle micro-expressions, followed by verbal communication. So, if we learn the art of reading those non-verbal cues, we can react according to the situation. Take eye contact for instance; if you are partner is unable to make eye contact with you, that implies shyness, discomfort, or deception. Similarly, there are several other gestures and expressions that imply different meanings, such as:

Body Language	
Open Posture	Arms uncrossed, facing the partner indicates openness and receptiveness.
Closed Posture	Crossing arms or legs might suggest defensiveness or discomfort.
Leaning In	It shows engagement and interest in the conversation.
Tone of Voice	
Soft and Warm	It reflects kindness, intimacy or affection.
Loud and Harsh	It indicates anger, frustration or annoyance.
Monotone	It can imply boredom, sadness or lack of interest.
Personal Space	
Invading Personal Space	Depending on context and relationship dynamics, it can indicate intimacy or aggression.
Maintaining Distance	It suggests respect for personal boundaries.
Touch	
Light Touch	It indicates care, affection or flirtation.
Strong Grip	It can convey confidence, sincerity or control.
Eye Movements	
Dilated Pupils	It indicates interest or attraction.
Avoiding Eye Contact	It can imply dishonesty, guilt or discomfort.

The table above only explains some of the more common body language signs; there are several other gestures and expressions that you can read on a human face. Better self-awareness and emotional intelligence can significantly help you recognize more of the non-verbal cues. Suppose that you and your partner are attending a social event together. As the evening progresses, you notice that your partner is sitting quietly, avoiding eye contact and fidgeting with their hands. If you notice these non-verbal cues in your partner, it may be an indication that they are feeling uneasy or overwhelmed in the social setting. To understand and support them, you might choose to approach them, express empathy, and suggest taking a break together or finding a quieter space. This demonstrates your attentiveness to their non-verbal cues and your willingness to understand and respond to their emotional state without relying solely on verbal communication.

Understanding the Love Language

According to various psychologists and relationship experts, another important language that you need to master in your communication with your partner is the language of love. People have different ways of expressing and receiving love. There are five primary love languages:

1. Words of affirmation

2. Acts of service

3. Receiving gifts

4. Spending quality time

5. Physical touch.

Everyone has a dominant love language through which they best express or understand and feel loved. In relationships, expressing love and appreciation in your partner's preferred love language can enhance your emotional connection and satisfaction. When you recognize and value each other's efforts in the specific way they understand love, you can create a positive and supportive atmosphere, fostering teamwork and mutual support.

For instance, if your partner's love language is acts of service then you will find them most happy or feeling loved when you help. Then, start doing that more often. Whether it is running errands or making breakfast, do whatever makes your partner feel loved. Similarly, tell your partner about your love language which can be words of affirmation of appreciation, and in this way your partner can reciprocate your love through your favorite love language.

While communicating in your desired love languages, it is also important to share words of appreciation for each other's efforts and input. If your partner recognizes your love language and makes an effort to express appreciation in words, then you appreciate their effort in return. Instead of simply enjoying the breakfast you prepare, your partner should tell you how much they appreciate your effort and skill in the kitchen.

When you start appreciating each other in your preferred love languages, you create a positive atmosphere in your home. Your verbal appreciation makes your partner feel valued and loved, enhancing your emotional connection. Your helpful gestures make your partner feel supported and cared for, strengthening your bond as a couple.

Problem-Solving As a Team

A relationship is more like a partnership; you both are in this together. So, whatever you do, you will have to do it as a team. It is the conscious efforts and consistent input of both partners that nurture the relationship, so never take the responsibility of solving a problem on your own or putting it all on your partner. It is intelligent to sit together, assess the situation, look for solutions together, and then develop a strategy that works for both of you. To do this, there are several expert-suggested techniques that I think you should definitely apply:

1. Collaborative Problem-Solving

Dr. Susan Heitler, a clinical psychologist, advocated this technique which mainly emphasizes teamwork and mutual understanding when addressing issues within a relationship. Finding a solution to a problem together develops a deeper bond between two partners.

2. Identify The Problem

The first step in this process is to discuss the problem at hand. Let's say you are both having money problems and spending more than what you earn. The best way to work on it as a team is to specify a time to sit together and list all the money problems you both think you are having. When you discuss the problems, make sure to keep the blame game and accusations aside. You are sitting together to work out a solution and blaming isn't going to help. Be specific and honest with each other during this conversation. Once you both pinpoint the problems and their causes, get ready for the next step!

3. Brainstorming Solutions Together

Once the problem is defined, engage in a joint brainstorming session with your partner to come up with potential solutions.

This means creative thinking and considering various options. While doing this, create an open and non-judgmental space where both of you can suggest possible solutions. Jot down a list of all the ideas without criticism. Be open to considering unconventional or unexpected suggestions. Brainstorming together allows for a diverse range of solutions to be explored. If either of you need time to think about the solution, give each other the desired time and then resume this conversation.

4. Evaluate And Choose a Practical Resolution

The next step is to weigh the pros and cons of all the suggested solutions. Again, listen to each other without judgment and keep your personal biases away. Just think about what is in the best interest of you and your partner. Evaluate each option to determine its feasibility, effectiveness, and mutually agreed remedy. The ultimate goal is to reach a solution that both partners are comfortable with. Discuss the practicality, fairness, and long-term implications of each option. Aim for a resolution that addresses the concerns of both partners and is realistic in the given context. It might involve compromising or finding a middle ground that accommodates both perspectives.

5. Implement And Reassess

Once you both agree on a solution, you can then implement the chosen course of action. After a certain period of time, reassess the situation to evaluate the effectiveness of the resolution and make adjustments if required. While doing that, make sure to discuss the next course of action with your partner. Put the chosen solution into action and give it a fair trial period. Regularly communicate and evaluate how the solution is working for both of you. If it proves to be ineffective or needs adjustments, collaborate again to find a better solution.

Author's Note

I hope you are enjoying the book so far and have started to see some value in the key steps you have undertaken up to this point.

I would greatly appreciate your support by leaving this book an honest review on Amazon. Reviews are hard to come by and they are critical to authors such as myself.

I read every review, and your valuable feedback not only provides insights into your thoughts on this book but helps me improve.

It also really helps others to discover this book.

Thank you so much
Rohini Heendeniya

You can use the QR codes below to leave a review on Amazon US or Amazon UK, or you can go to your Amazon Orders page where you can click on the link to write a review on the book.

Amazon US

Amazon UK

PART III

Turning Conflicts into Opportunities Through Emotional Intelligence

Chapter 6

GRACEFUL DISAGREEMENTS

Transforming Arguments Into Understanding

What happens when you argue with your partner? Do you engage in a heated discussion? Do either one of you stop talking or does it escalate into something loud and chaotic?

These are some of the possible ways a disagreement could go. But in every possible situation, there is always some unmet need or a problem that needs to be taken care of. The problem is when we focus too much on the issue and focus too little on a resolution - that's when a disagreement can intensify. Conflicts are neither good nor bad, what makes them potentially harmful to a relationship is the way they are dealt with. So, in this chapter, we will be making sense of it all and discover expert suggested methods of turning disagreements into a pathway of understanding and harmony.

The Inevitability of Conflicts and the Role of Emotional Intelligence

"Conflict can and should be handled constructively; when it is, relationships benefit. Conflict avoidance is not *the hallmark of*

a good relationship. On the contrary, it is a symptom of serious problems and poor communication." – Harriet B. Braiker

Conflicts are a blessing in disguise! The way I see conflicts, and Dudley D. Cahn and Ruth Anna Abigail also share the same view, is that they are a normal and inevitable part of life. When a conflict arises between two partners it creates an avenue to share honest opinions and thoughts. It allows the couple to talk about their feelings and ideals.

However, problems may arise when either of the partners hesitates to seize this opportunity or simply chooses to avoid it just because they don't see eye-to-eye. When a conflict is left unchecked and ignored it tends to fester and it grows into some level of resentment, discontent, and distance between the partners. No two people can agree on every possible matter, disagreement is a natural occurrence. Once we realize this very fact, we start looking for constructive and healthy ways to deal with conflicts instead of avoiding them. That is the first step toward having a successful interpersonal relationship.

Research has proved that emotional intelligence gives us the insight to navigate through all our conflicts. A research study in 2020 set out to explore the impact of emotional intelligence on relationship satisfaction levels and the stress management process in a romantic relationship (dyadic coping). Now, according to Guy Bodenmann's Systemic Transactional Model (STM), there are three types of dyadic coping: Positive, Common and Negative. In positive dyadic coping, partners reduce each other's stress by sharing responsibilities and contributing to the coping process. In a common or joint dyadic process, the partners jointly work together to reduce stress. Whereas in negative dyadic coping, partners offer insufficient support and hostile intervention. According to another 2020 study, emotional intelligence is positively related to positive and common dyadic coping mechanisms. So, when couples have higher emotional intelligence, they are more open to offering support and sharing responsibility during stressful situations.

A study conducted by the University of California, Berkeley, proved that people who have high levels of EI are good at turning arguments into constructive discussions. This is solely because with higher EI comes the ability to understand and manage emotions while empathizing with the feelings of others. So, when in a heated argument, rationality takes the backseat and tempers flare up, emotional intelligence can help a person de-escalate the situation by expressing empathy, actively listening, and finding common ground. Through the lens of EI, you seek conflicts not as battles to be won but as opportunities to develop understanding and foster growth.

How Do You Engage in Conflict?

As individuals, we all grow up to develop various coping mechanisms, and not all of us engage in conflicts the same way. For instance, between me and my partner, I am the one who used to avoid addressing the conflicts, until I discovered the power of collaboration and open communication. According to Richard E. Walton and Robert B. McKersie's 1965 model of ABCs of Conflict, there are three distinct patterns of behavior that people show in a conflict:

- Avoiders

- Battlers

- Collaborators

According to this model, Avoiders simply act to avoid or ignore the conflict at hand. The Battlers in a conflict turn out to be defensive, sarcastic, and hurting. Whereas the Collaborators are the ones who sit with others to seek a win-win solution to the conflict. Let's use this simple questionnaire to assess in which category you fall.

Exercise: ABC of Conflict

Answer the following statements, using the scale below to rate the degree to which each statement applies to you, and how you typically behave when engaged in conflict with your partner.

1 = Strongly Disagree
2 = Disagree
3 = Neutral
4 = Agree
5 = Strongly Agree

Using the scale above, against each numbered statement below, decide how much you agree or disagree with how this applies to you:

When I start to engage in a conflict, I...

1. ... keep the conflict to myself to avoid rocking the boat.

2. ... do my best to stay away from disagreements that arise.

3. ... avoid the individual with whom I'm having the conflict.

4. ... leave the room to avoid dealing with the issue.

5. ... shut down and shut up in order to get it over with as quickly as possible.

6. ... keep my disagreements to myself.

7. ... don't let up until I win.

8. ... see it as an opportunity to get what I want.

9. ... create a strategy to ensure my successful outcome.

10. ... do my best to win.

11. ... won't back down unless I get what I want.

12. ... take no prisoners.

13. ... try to find a solution that works for everyone.

14. ... try to find a solution that is beneficial for those involved.

15. ... collaborate with others to find an outcome OK for everyone.

16. ... find solutions that satisfy everyone's expectations.

17. ... try to integrate everyone's ideas to come up with the best solution for everyone.

18. ... openly raise everyone's concerns to ensure the best outcome possible.

Now add your choices against the corresponding statement numbers below and total each set of scores:

Avoiders:

To assess whether you are an Avoider or not: 1____, 4____, 7____, 10____, 13____, 16____, TOTAL = _____
Out of a potential total score of 30, if the score is below 15, then you are not much of an Avoider. Scores over 15 mean you are an Avoider.

Battlers:

To assess whether you are a Battler or not: 2____, 5____, 8____, 11____, 14____, 17____, TOTAL = _____
Out of a potential total score of 30, if the score is below 15, then you are not much of a Battler. Scores over 15 mean you are a Battler.

Collaborators:

To assess whether you are a Collaborator or not: 3____, 6____, 9____, 12____, 15____, 18____, TOTAL = _____
Out of a potential total score of 30, if the score is below 15, then you are not much of a Collaborator. Scores over 15 mean you are a Collaborator.

From the results of the above exercise, you can assess the type of conflict management style you engage in. When you are an Avoider or Battler, managing conflict to gain a positive outcome becomes a challenge. So, the next few sections of this chapter will help you learn effective techniques to manage all your conflicts and achieve positive outcomes.

Can Conflict Bring Partners Closer?

Yes, if handled correctly and resolved through positive approaches (shared in the next section). Conflicts can even increase closeness and intimacy between partners. The research study conducted by Anne Milek and her colleagues at the University of Zurich, explored the factors that contribute to intimacy in relationships, focusing on how couples handle intra-dyadic stress (stress related to each other). The findings of the study suggested that in relationships marked by stress related to each other, addressing and resolving problems may not only prevent a decrease in intimacy but could potentially increase it. The research highlighted that constant romantic interaction is not necessary for emotional closeness, but spending enough quality time together, especially during weekends, enables couples to navigate occasional conflicts and return to a more satisfying emotional state.

Healthy vs Unhealthy Conflicts

The differentiation between healthy and unhealthy conflicts can be found in the perception and expression of emotions. How we choose to communicate our feelings shapes our disagreements. Let me list some of the defining key characteristics of a healthy conflict here. You can use this list as a yardstick to assess which type of conflict you engage in and then you can resort to appropriate conflict resolution techniques (shared later in this chapter) to enhance your relationship and strengthen the bond with your partner:

- **Open Communication:**
  All healthy conflicts have open communication. You open up when you feel that you are not being judged for your opinions and feel safe to share your thoughts. When you can easily communicate your feelings to one another, you can engage in a healthy conflict.

- **Dialogue With Respect:**
  The next major ingredient of a healthy conflict recipe is having a respectful dialogue. Even when you disagree with your partner, you can still choose a respectable means of sharing your feelings without personal attacks and playing the blame game.

- **Listen Before You React!**
  When you actively listen to other people's concerns without interrupting or storming out, then you give yourself the due time to process the information and offer necessary solutions to the problem at hand.

- **Empathy:**
  Remember how we talked about empathy as a secret ingredient of building strong connections? In case of any conflict, empathy also serves as a bridge to counter

the differences and bring both partners to a table. Only through empathy, can you choose to respect your partner's differing views and understand them.

- **Constructive Problem-Solving:**
Once the problem at hand is understood and communicated, the next crucial element is resorting to constructive problem-solving. This means that the two of you decide to sit together, discuss the details, the differences, possible options, and reach a win-win solution.

- **Clear Expression of Needs:**
At the heart of every conflict, there is always some sort of need that is not being met. According to Marshall Rosenberg, relational needs can be categorized into the need for autonomy, celebration, play, spiritual communion, physical nurturance, integrity, and interdependence. When any of those needs are not met, then the healthy way to deal with the matter is to express and share with the partner.

- **Maintaining Emotional Control:**
Now, I know that maintaining emotional control during a heated argument is not possible, but we can try to employ techniques to stay calm and composed, at least that's what makes a conflict healthy. Chapter 2 discusses various techniques to recognize emotional patterns and regulate them in varying situations. You may find it useful to go back and review those techniques at this point.

- **Focus on The Issue, Not The Person:**
When you focus on the person and forget the issue at hand, you indulge in personal attacks and blame games. The goal always must be to find the relevant solution to the conflict, not to target your partner.

- **Learning and Growth:**
For a conflict to be healthy, it is important for both partners involved to see it as a source of learning and growth. Both partners can learn from each other's diverging views and learn to work ways around those differences.

- **Resolution and Closure:**
  A healthy conflict never lingers on. When you discuss your issues with your partner when conflict arises and work together to find a win-win solution, you can resolve the conflict and find closure in a timely way. In doing so, you don't end up carrying past grievances or grudges against one another.

- **Adaptability:**
  Healthy conflicts create room for adaptability and flexibility. In such conflicts, you show your willingness to adjust your expectations and behaviors to accommodate your partner's needs and preferences, which significantly helps strengthen your bond.

The Unhealthy Conflicts

There often comes a time when you start off a casual conversation with your partner, one thing leads to another and suddenly you find yourself in the middle of a heated disagreement. You say something hurtful, your partner says something more distressing in return and you ask yourself "How did we get here?" This can happen when either one or both of you lack the emotional intelligence to express your emotions, feelings, and intentions in the right manner. Thus, the negativity in the discussion outweighs the positivity and it turns the whole conflict into an unhealthy one. If you want to assess the characteristics of an unhealthy conflict and their respective impact on a relationship, then here is a list that can help you:

- **Criticism:**
  It is one thing to complain about a matter, but when a person criticizes their partner, it may include some negative judgment of their character or behavior. If you were to say something such as, "You always prioritize work over our time together. You are so self-centered and do not care about my needs." - Though the statement is about your partner not meeting your needs, it is packed in the ugly-looking wrapper of judgment. Whereas the same thought can be conveyed as, "Your work is taking most of your time, so much so that we don't get to spend some quality time together, and I really want us to spend some good time together." Now, this statement conveys the concerns and expresses the

unmet needs without any hint of criticism.

- **Defensiveness:**
  When we act defensively in a conflict, we deny the responsibility and simply focus on protecting ourselves without considering our partners' feelings and emotions. Through defensiveness, we do not leave room for adaptability and change. So instead of reaching a sound solution to a problem, we get stuck in the negative cycle of the blame game. For instance, if one partner says, "You never help with the household chores," a defensive response to this could be "Well, I would help if you didn't nag me all the time. It is not just my responsibility." Now, you can see how this response can initiate a trigger reaction.

- **Stonewalling:**
  During stonewalling, one of the partners withdraws from the interaction, shuts down, or refuses to engage in the conversation during a conflict. This behavior makes it almost possible to reach a resolution. According to "The Horsemen of Apocalypse" model presented by Dr. Gottman, this type of behavior can be a death note for a relationship and hence must be avoided.

- **Unresolved Issues:**
  During an unhealthy conflict, partners often bring up past grievances instead of discussing the issues at hand. They then get stuck in a cycle of discussing unresolved grievances, so they don't mutually find an agreeable solution to the most recent problem, and issues continue to pile up.

- **Lack of Empathy:**
  When partners show the inability to understand each other's perspective and dismiss each other's feelings, the conflict becomes damaging and unhealthy. A lack of empathy makes conflict damaging to a relationship.

Co-dependency In Relationships

While we are on the subject of unhealthy conflicts, I cannot move forward without addressing another major issue that several couples face without realizing it - and that is 'co-dependency.' It is a dysfunctional pattern of behavior with a one-sided dynamic where one partner relies excessively on the other for emotional support, validation, or a sense of identity. This pattern of behavior can negatively impact both partners involved and the overall health of the relationship. There is a lack of personal boundaries, fear of abandonment, and little or no open or honest communication in a codependent relationship. People suffering from co-dependency issues may often absolve their partners of their responsibilities and later feel sorry for themselves. According to research, co-dependency issues develop due to negative past experiences or when children learn such traits from their parents. The good news is that any person with co-dependency issues can work on their behavioral patterns, unlearn them, and learn new ones to rebalance the relationship dynamics. The only way to accomplish this is by mastering emotional intelligence. If co-dependency issues sound familiar to you and evoke a feeling that you do exhibit such traits, then here are some effective techniques to employ:

1. Explore yourself and become self-aware. The self-reflection techniques shared in Chapter 1 of this book will greatly help any co-dependent person in this regard. When you become more aware of your emotions, thoughts, and values, you realize that the power of controlling them lies in your hands and you stop relying excessively on your partner.

2. Start incorporating emotional regulation exercises like mindful walking, yoga, meditation, and deep breathing, on a regular basis.

3. Use positive affirmations to boost your confidence and stay focused on your goals in life. Consider yourself as the master of your mind and exercise your power over your thoughts and actions.

Only by becoming more emotionally intelligent, empowered, and self-aware can you overcome your vulnerabilities and establish relations with well-defined and healthy boundaries.

Turning Heated Fights into Graceful Disagreements

Research was conducted on newlywed couples to assess the success of their marriages based on how they communicated during conflicts. The study showed that the strongest variable of a happy and lasting marriage was the expression of positive emotions during conflicts. Couples in successful marriages demonstrated the ability to add positive comments, or light-heartedness during stressful times, effectively de-escalating conflicts. The findings highlighted the importance of adding positive interactions in relationships to enhance conflict resolution and overall satisfaction. That is the essence of having graceful disagreements! If you equip yourself with empathy and the ability to comprehend emotions, you learn to tackle disagreements without letting the negativity get in the way. Knowing the concerns of several couples around the world, I would like to list some effective conflict resolution techniques according to the purpose they serve!

Understanding and Dealing with Emotional Baggage

To navigate through impending conflicts, the first and foremost strategy is to deal with the emotional baggage. If something has been bothering you or your partner for quite some time, then it will keep brewing toward conflict if left unaddressed. So, it is imperative to work on past grievances and find closure before moving forward. Here is how you can do it:

- **Active Listening:**
  Sit down with your partner and spare some time to listen to each other's concerns without judgment. It is best for couples to schedule a weekly session of listening to each other so that both partners get sufficient time to address problems on a regular basis.

- **Open Communication:**
  Always keep the line of communication open between you and your partner. Say, you are mad about your partner forgetting your anniversary and you want them to realize it on their own. Still, I would recommend

sharing whatever is bothering you and telling them about the level of hurt it caused so that your partner would feel the need to rectify the mistake.

- **Seek Professional Help:**
  Sometimes, the emotional baggage gets too heavy to carry. In such situations, it is best to consult a certified therapist and share the past experiences and their impact. Therapists offer personalized support that would help you deal with unhealed traumas and offer support to unlearn unhealthy behavioral patterns.

In The Middle of an Argument

It is one thing to learn and practice conflict management techniques when you are calm and in a good mood. However, in the middle of an argument when heat flares up, it is difficult to think straight and talk rationally. That is why I suggest the following three-step formula to dial down the heat when things start to escalate.

- **Take a Break and Calm Down:**
  "If you care about the relationship, then think before you speak. Because when you blurt, you hurt." -Dr. Rhoberta Shaler
  Though you feel the need to address the issue immediately, when emotions escalate and rationality leaves the conversation, it is better to take a break and discuss the matter later. It is an effective way to give yourself and your partner the necessary time to cool down and think rationally. But remember to take a break with the consent of your partner. If you leave the conversation without saying anything, that will aggravate the conflict. You can suggest taking a break during a heated argument by saying something along the lines of:

  "Hey, I have noticed that things are getting a bit intense, and I want us to communicate better. How about we take a break when emotions start to feel overwhelming? It is not about avoiding the conversation but giving ourselves a chance to cool down and gather our thoughts. What do you think?"

Once you both cool off, you can continue the conversation by sharing your respective opinions.

- **Use "I" Statements to Express Feelings Instead of Blaming:**
Marshall Rosenberg, the father of nonviolent communication suggests that there is an inherent problem in using "You" statements during conflicts. Such statements carry moralistic judgment and accuse others of the emotions you feel. Though their actions may make you feel a certain way, the power of controlling your emotions lies in your hands. The best way to address this is to use the "I" statements. Using such statements, you convey your concerns without blaming your partner, so the conflict does not escalate rather you open the channel of communication. For instance, if you feel like your partner has not been giving you much time, instead of saying, *"You don't care about me or you never have time for me,"* you can say *"I have noticed that I have been feeling a bit neglected lately, and I wanted to talk to you about it. I feel like we could spend more quality time together. How do you feel about that?"* With such a statement, no room for confusion is left and you express your emotions without pointing fingers at your partner.

- **Develop a Signal or Code to Indicate Escalating Emotions:**
You and your partner should come up with a system to de-escalate emotions during a conflict. It works best if you assign a sign or symbol. It can be any non-verbal or verbal sign that would indicate that you want to slow down and reengage in a constructive dialogue later.

- **Stop Misinterpreting Your Partner's Feelings:**
Guesswork never works well for any relationship. Let's be honest, we are not playing "Who guessed it right?" We humans are designed to learn and understand through communication. So, instead of making assumptions about your partner's feelings and emotions, take a moment to ask what is bothering them.

- **Ask Clarifying Questions Instead of Making Assumptions:**
Let's assume for a second that your partner seems distant, and you are unsure if something is bothering

them. Instead of assuming: *"You're mad at me, aren't you?"* use a clarifying question to ask what is bothering them: *"I have noticed you seem a bit quiet today. Is everything okay, or is there something on your mind?"* In this way, you don't limit the conversation but open it up and create an atmosphere of understanding.

- **Practice Empathy by Seeing The Situation from Your Partner's Perspective:**
  Remember how we talked about empathy as a valuable tool to understand your partner's perspective? Well, if you want to keep your disagreement graceful and solution-oriented, you have to show empathy toward their emotions and feelings. Let's see how positively impactful a statement becomes when you add a dash of empathy to it! Say your partner is stressed due to a high workload, there are two ways to approach this situation:
  o <u>Without Empathy</u>: *"You are always stressed. It's not that big of a deal."*
  o <u>With Empathy</u>: *"I can see that this project is causing you a lot of stress. How can I support you during this busy time?"*
  The idea is to put yourself in your partner's shoes and feel how they would be feeling before commenting on a situation. Trust me! A lot of conflicts end before even getting started when couples start empathizing with one another.

- **Reduce Defensiveness:**
  When people are tied in a romantic relationship, they become a team that must collaborate with one another to find resolutions to their individual and collective problems. But when either one of the partners gets defensiveness during an argument, it shatters the idea of partnership, and they deny the responsibility to fixing things. The defensiveness may arise due to certain causes:

1. When a person is too perfectionist, the mere idea of making a mistake drives them crazy.

2. A person might have a childhood where they were punished for making mistakes and now they have developed a fear of making mistakes.

3. When a person is insecure about who they are and what they can do.

4. When a person is uncomfortable in feeling, admitting, and expressing emotions like shame, guilt, or embarrassment.

5. Defensiveness can be a symptom of an anxiety disorder.

Working on individual causes can help avoid defensiveness. For instance, for a perfectionist, understanding "to err is to human" could help them accept their own mistakes and learn from them. Once a person realizes that making mistakes is what makes us human, they overcome the fear of mistakes while dealing with insecurities through self-awareness.

- **Improve Expression of Feelings:**
  We fail to express a wide range of emotions simply because we lack the emotional vocabulary required for it. While communicating our feelings with our partner, whether negative or positive, it is important to be specific about them. In his work on non-violent communication, Rosenberg explored a similar dimension and expressed the view that identifying emotions and expressing them in specific words can help avoid a lot of confusion and misunderstanding that otherwise leads to conflicts. So instead of saying, *"I am not in the mood right now to argue with you,"* which would sound rude and dismissive to a partner, you can try specifying your feelings by saying, *"I am feeling a bit disheartened and frustrated because the project at work didn't unfold as I had hoped."* This statement explains the whole range and intensity of your emotions which can help your partner assess the situation and understand it better.

- **Decision-Making During Emotional Situations:**
  They say, "Never make a decision in anger," and that makes sense. When your mind is clouded with negative emotions, every decision you make gets the brunt of it. So, if there is a matter that requires a decision, involve your partner in it. If the argument escalates, simply postpone the decision for a short time, until

you both are ready to talk through it rationally. If you have important or time-sensitive decisions to make and nothing is working out despite your efforts, then it could be useful to seek external help from a relationship expert. A professional therapist can intervene and give their neutral input to help both of you understand each other, analyze the problems objectively, and reach a mutually agreed solution.

- **Positively Approach Criticism:**
  The moment you start seeing criticism as an opportunity to learn and grow, the world starts looking brighter and more colorful. If a person expresses their desire to spend more time with their partner, it simply indicates that there is an unfulfilled need that has to be taken care of. To resolve the problem, the partner must reflect on their actions and identify areas to work on - that could include better time management or planning a holiday to spend more time with their loved one.

To sum it up, how we choose to engage with our partner during a conflict primarily decides the nature of the bond we share. Brushing matters under the carpet, lack of communication, defensiveness, and disregarding your partner's emotions can escalate the conflicts. So, the effective way to approach a conflict positively is to choose empathy, open communication, collaboration, and emotional regulation to learn and grow from your mistakes.

Chapter 7

POST CONFLICT HEALING

Rebuilding Trust and Love

"Hold no grudges and practice forgiveness. This is the key to having peace in all your relationships." – Wayne Dyer

Every conflict leaves you with a series of valuable lessons to learn from. When couples indulge in the post-conflict healing process it transforms their relationship and their bond grows stronger. As Ursula K. Le Guin said, *"Love doesn't just sit there, like a stone. It has to be made, like bread, remade all the time, made new."* That love and connection is remade through the conscious efforts of both partners towards rebuilding the trust. It is a whole process of acknowledging vulnerability, accepting weaknesses, and sharing the willingness to support one another no matter what. In this chapter, we are moving one step ahead of conflict resolution and stepping towards identifying growth opportunities, creating stronger connections, and fostering resilience.

Authentic Apology

"Never let a problem to be solved become more important than a person to be loved." - Leo F. Buscagalia

The process of healing begins with authentic apologies after recognizing that conflicts are inevitable in any relationship. When we upset our partner or feel upset, a sincere apology becomes a bridge to healing. Receiving a genuine apology dissipates negative energy and creates room for forgiveness and the restoration of trust. It involves letting down our defenses and creating space for love to flow organically between partners.

So, what makes an apology authentic? It's sincerity! It takes a lot of introspection to analyze where you have done wrong and how you can genuinely fix things. Apologizing authentically is not only empowering but it also demonstrates the enhanced level of maturity and emotional understanding. It is an investment in the relationship's growth, to create a deeper connection which leads to a more profound level of intimacy.

On the other hand, an insincere apology does more harm than good. I have seen countless people using the same old "sorry" to an extent where the word just loses its meaning. If you really want to rebuild trust and rekindle your love, then focus on the Dos and Don'ts of apologizing to move past the conflict and step into the healing phase.

- **Don't Use Conditional Language:**
  "Ifs and that's" take all the value away from an apology. For instance, saying: "I am sorry if you were offended," simply indicates that you have no clue of your mistakes and you have no intention of taking the responsibility to settle the matter with your partner. Instead, use language that shows remorse and regret. You can say "I am sorry that I offended you and I am willing to make things better from now on." This statement shows the will to improve and change.

- **Never Minimize the Impact:**
  One of the most lethal forms of apology is when you use it to downplay the significance of the situation or the impact of your actions:

  Here is an example of a downplaying response:
  "I know I missed the event; I am sorry! But it is not that big of a deal. We can always celebrate later. Why are you making such a fuss about it?"

The same apology can be restructured as:
"I understand that missing the event was hurtful, and I know how important it must have been for you. I am truly sorry for not being there, and I recognize that my actions have caused disappointment. Let's talk about how I can make it up to you and make sure it doesn't happen again."

- **Don't Shift Blame:**
  It is tempting to shift the blame to an external factor like a situation or another person, but it makes you look insincere when you do that. An apology only appears genuine when a person takes full responsibility for causing the hurt. It is natural for our self-defense to kick in and we avoid taking the blame for our actions. But when we ask ourselves honest questions from a neutral standpoint, we can analyze the situation better. The trick is to stop seeing the conflict from your own perspective. Instead, think of yourself as a third person looking at you and your partner in conflict. Focus on the problem not the person, then you can fight the instinct of blaming your partner.

Show Through Action

An apology not backed by visible action can make you look insincere. If you don't have a clue what to do, then take advantage of open communication and ask your partner something like, "What is it that I can do to make things better?" The answer to this might guide you in the right direction.

Learn the Art of Letting Go

Post-conflict healing not only involves authentic and sincere apologies but also requires both partners to accept each other's apologies with an open mind and heart. I believe that accepting an apology requires far more courage than offering an apology, and it only becomes easier for us when we are in sync with our own emotions. When we develop higher levels of self-awareness and emotional intelligence, we understand that we all are susceptible to making mistakes. What matters is that we learn from them, leave the mistakes behind, and move on with the newfound awareness. Unresolved conflicts only add extra weight to the emotional baggage, so it is best to work on them, communicate with your partner, work on the solutions together, apologize forgive then start fresh. While you accept the apology, it is important to truly believe in it, without any hint of skepticism.

The Don'ts of Post-Conflict Healing

Once the conflict is over, you step into a dangerous territory. This time can be best utilized to strengthen the bond with your partner. But if you end up making some unintentional mistakes then a conflict may even leave behind some irreparable damage, which might negatively affect your relationship in the long run. Let me introduce you to the "Don'ts" of post-conflict healing! These are post-conflict behavioral patterns that I have found several couples falling into without being aware of. I would suggest you stay cautious and avoid repeating the same mistakes.

Never Act Like Nothing Happened:
Downplaying the emotions of your partner or yourself is not a wise move. Ignoring never works, it is the same as brushing things under the carpet. On the surface, it may seem like everything has gotten better with your partner, but the unresolved conflict continues to brew feelings of dissatisfaction and a little resentment.

Don't Broadcast Your Conflict in Public:
This major mistake may prove detrimental in the long run. If you feel like you want to share your feelings with an outsider, then reach out to a therapist or relationship counselor. But never make the mistake of sharing the intimate details of your conflict on social media, with family or friends. The breach of privacy is threatening to the relationship.

Don't Let Too Much Time Pass:
The idea that "things will get better with time" is completely flawed and it only gets better when we consciously make an effort to work on them. When you spend a considerable duration of time without resolving the conflict, you create a gap between you and your partner, which allows negative emotions, confusion, and misunderstanding to step in.

Don't Bring Up the Argument in the Future:
Once you have worked on a conflict and exchanged apologies, avoid bringing up the same arguments in the future. When you continually revisit past arguments, it prevents any forward progress. It is similar to constantly digging up the roots of a plant which hinders the growth of your relationship.

Don't Say You Didn't Mean It:
When we dismiss hurtful words as unintentional it downplays their impact. It is the same as trying to take back rocks thrown into a lake; the ripples are already there, and the effect remains.

Don't Have Makeup Sex if You Don't Want To:
It is futile to engage in physical intimacy when you don't feel a genuine emotional connection and it can create a false sense of conflict resolution. This is like putting a band-aid over a chronic wound without fixing the underlying issues and expecting them to get resolved.

Don't Focus Solely on the Cause:
Sometimes we can fixate on the specific trigger of the fight which often overshadows the deeper emotional needs or communication issues. If you had a fight about your partner arriving late to a family event, then there must be some underlying unmet needs that require attention. So, look for the deeper issues, not the apparent cause.

Don't Give the Silent Treatment:
The silent treatment is often the death of a meaningful and healthy relationship. It aggravates the conflict, makes the partner uncomfortable, and paves the way for misunderstandings.

Learning from Mistakes

Conflicts help us learn from our past mistakes. They are the wake-up call to reflect and work on our mindset and behavior patterns to take the relationship in the right direction. Every little fight or disagreement allows you to understand your partner better if you use them as an opportunity for open communication and sharing of feelings.

"People are naturally imperfect. No matter what your relationship, whether parent, child, friend, or lover, there will

always be mistakes on both sides. It's how we choose to accept the flaws of the people who surround us that determines our peace."   – Kate J. Squires

Reflect Together:
Take time together to reflect on the mistake or conflict. Discuss what went wrong, and how it made each of you feel, and identify the contributing factors. This joint reflection promotes understanding and helps both of you gain insights into the situation.

Identify Patterns:
Look for patterns or recurring issues in the relationship. Identifying patterns helps you understand if there are underlying issues that need addressing. Recognizing these patterns is the first step toward breaking negative cycles.

Establish Clear Expectations:
Communicate expectations and boundaries in your relationship. Discuss what both of you value, need, and hope for, ensuring that you are on the same page. Establishing clear expectations minimizes misunderstandings and potential conflicts.

Celebrate Growth:
Acknowledge and celebrate the growth and positive changes that result from learning from mistakes. This reinforces the idea that challenges are growth opportunities and strengthens the bond between you and your partner.

Forgive and Let Go:
Practice forgiveness. Holding onto resentment only perpetuates negative emotions and hinders personal and relational development. Forgiving doesn't mean forgetting, but it allows for moving forward without carrying the weight of past mistakes.

Commit to Continuous Improvement:
Recognize that personal and relational growth is an ongoing process. Commit to learning from mistakes continually, adapting to new challenges, and evolving together as a couple.

Demonstrating Change Through Actions:
Actions speak louder than words. Show your sincerity by making positive changes in your behavior. Consistently implement the

solutions you discussed with your partner. An example could be, "*I'm committed to being more mindful of my words and actions. Let's work together to make our communication healthier.*"

Giving Time and Space:
Understand that healing takes time. Give your partner the space they need to process their emotions. Be patient and demonstrate your commitment to positive change over time. Acknowledge their need for space, saying, "*I understand if you need time to process this. I'm here for you when you are ready to talk.*"

Part IV

*Parenting with Emotional Intelligence
– How Your Relationship Shapes Your
Child's World*

Chapter 8

CO-PARENTING MASTERY

Nurturing Children with Love and Understanding

"Emotional intelligence begins to develop in the earliest years. All the small exchanges children have with their parents, teachers, and with each other carry emotional messages." - Daniel Goleman

Emotionally intelligent kids grow up to be secure, grounded and confident adults. Just recall your childhood, the teenage and those high school years, what comes to mind? Many people remember the challenges of their childhood without emotional coaching, such as struggling with their emotions, difficulty reading others, and not knowing how or when to react in a situation. Kids tend to learn everything about emotions from parents, primary caregivers and other close influences. Parents play the most crucial part in this. So, as an adult, it is not only crucial for us to enhance our ability to process emotions but also to infuse the same skills in our children. By doing so, we equip them to successfully navigate through all realms of life, from personal relationships to their careers.

Balancing Empathy and Discipline

The sweet spot of parenting lies in the balance between empathy and discipline. When children misbehave or throw tantrums, their frustration is frequently more than just not receiving a favored toy or visiting their favorite place. These behaviors usually stem from deeper issues, with underlying emotions driving their actions. When we neglect the cause and try to fix things by only disciplining the kids then it causes more frustration and creates a wide emotional gap between parents and the children. This is where EI comes to the rescue, as it equips us with the power of empathy, understanding, and better communication skills to approach our children. It lets us listen to them actively and help them deal with their problems.

Common Language for Co-Parents

"Often parents communicate most effectively with their children by the way they listen to and address each other. Their conversations showing gentleness and love are heard by our ever-alert, impressionable children." — Marvin J. Ashton

Parenting is like a wild ride that takes you through several twists and turns. Only the strength of the relationship between the parents can help them cope with the challenges that come their way. From opting for the appropriate parenting style to communicating with the kids, both parents must work as a team to raise emotionally sound children. In this whole co-parenting equation, one valuable skill set that can help parents navigate through the unknown waters is their combined emotional intelligence. It acts as a common parenting language that brings the parents closer to one another and helps them harmonize their co-parenting dynamic.

Revolutionizing Relationships and Nurturing Emotional Growth

When emotional intelligence is incorporated in parenting it can revolutionize not only the relationship between co-parents but also contribute to the child's emotional growth. For instance, if your child is struggling with school, being an emotionally intelligent parent, you would not only focus on academic performance but also address your child's emotions and stressors. You might create an open space for your child to express their feelings, providing support and guidance. This approach both strengthens the parent-child bond and teaches them valuable emotional regulation skills, setting the stage for healthy emotional development.

Raising Emotionally Intelligent Kids

A study published in the Journal of Applied School Psychology found that students who received EI education showed a significant increase in pro-social behavior and decrease in disruptive behavior. Teaching our kids about emotions is a way to give them the superpower to socialize well and face every challenge with an open mind. Say your child comes home from school all excited about a project or upset about a fight with a friend. You can use this as an opportunity to learn about their emotions and connect with them at a deeper level. By using these everyday moments, you can dive into their feelings. You can say things like, *"I can see you are really happy about your project. That's awesome!"* or *"It sounds like you are quite upset about what happened with your friend. Let's talk about how you feel and how we can make things better."*

The important fact is that you are the superhero who is going to model emotional intelligence and show them how to handle life's twists and turns with grace, empathy, and bounce-back resilience. When you deal with stress or a setback and let them in on how you are working through it, then you teach them valuable lessons. If you make mistakes, that is okay. Just admit it, talk about how you are sorting out your feelings, and show them it is okay to make mistakes. By doing this, you are creating a highly supportive and safe space where your child feels comfortable expressing their feelings without worrying about being judged. It sets the stage for them to develop their emotional smarts and helps them rock their relationships and tackle life like a boss.

Understanding Child Development Stages

Children experience emotions differently throughout their

developmental phases. Their brain constantly grows and rewires according to the environment they are raised. It is their age that defines the capacity of their cognitive function. You cannot communicate with a five-year-old kid the same way you communicate with a toddler. So, it is imperative to understand the requirements of their particular age and developmental stage, and then develop an effective strategy to coach them in emotional intelligence.

Infancy (0-2 years):
During this stage, babies pick up their surrounding energies. Their emotional intelligence starts with recognizing basic needs. As a parent, your job is to decode their cries, learn what soothes them, and create that early bond. For instance, if a baby is fussy, you must learn to differentiate between hunger cries, tired cries, and everything in between. Your appropriate response builds a foundation of trust and security.

Toddlerhood (2-3 years):
Once a child becomes a toddler, they start discovering independence and a range of emotions. They might start throwing tantrums as a way to express their frustration. Sometimes, our reaction to their expression helps them learn new behaviors. At this stage, it is crucial to deal with a balance of gentle discipline and love. Since a child in this age range cannot express emotions through verbal means, you will have to do the talking for them. Here, your role is not just comforting your child but teaching simple ways to express feelings: saying, "I see you are upset; it is okay to be mad" helps them associate words with emotions.

Preschool (3-5 years):
Kids become emotional sponges by the time they enter preschool. They quickly pick up behaviors, mimic them, and start understanding more complex feelings. This is the prime time to introduce emotions to your kids. You can introduce the concept of empathy by saying, *How do you think your friend feels when you share your toys? How would you feel?* At this stage, children learn most through creative means, so using short stories, and colorful pictures to explain emotions to them can be highly effective.

Early Childhood (6-8 years):
By the time children turn 6 years old, they start becoming more self-aware. This is the stage where you help them unlock the

power of self. They develop a sense of self and understand others' perspectives. Emotional intelligence can be infused to help them recognize and manage their emotions. If a child is feeling left out, you can guide them in expressing their feelings to friends and offer them a supportive environment.

Middle Childhood (9-11 years):
This is the age where children can learn to regulate their emotions. Using problem-solving skills and targeted activities you can teach them to manage stress, communicate effectively, and channel their emotions in appropriate ways. For example, if they are upset about a school project, it would be wise to discuss a step-by-step plan with them and show them how to manage pressure.

Adolescence (12-18 years):
Kids experience drastic changes when they enter the adolescence stage. Teenagers go through a series of emotional changes, they discover their identity and independence at this stage, which can be pretty overwhelming for them. The world starts shifting for a kid when they become a teenager, so they need the most support at this time. If you see them facing peer pressure, then help them discuss alternative responses and guide them to make healthier decisions by regulating their emotions.

Knowing all the above-mentioned stages helps you tailor your approach to what your child needs at each phase. It gives you the understanding that what worked during the toddler tantrum phase might not be effective during the teenage angst era. Being aware of these developmental milestones lets you be proactive, shaping an emotionally intelligent person who can navigate life's highs and lows with resilience and empathy. It is all about knowing how to speak their emotional language at each chapter of their growth. This understanding also helps us to grow as parents as well. Raising children is a whole new experience and it requires constant character evolution to support them effectively at every stage of their lives.

Emotion Coaching

You are the emotion coach for your child. Their attachment style, communication technique, and expressions are all shaped by your actions. They learn how to react to a situation based on your responses and the strategies you employ. It makes a great difference how we as adults approach situations and tackle them. Let me explain with an example here!

Consider two children, Sarah and Emily. They are raised in two different households. Sarah's parents haven't explored the power of EI to develop their parenting skills, whereas Emily's parents are more self-aware and employ emotion coaching to raise the kids. Both Emily and Sarah are upset about not getting invited to a friend's party. Let's see how Sarah's parent would address the situation:

Sarah:
Mom, I'm so upset. My friend didn't invite me to her birthday party.

Parent:
Oh, come on, Sarah, it is just a party. You are overreacting. Stop being so sensitive.

Sarah:
But Mom, I thought we were friends. It really hurts.

Parent:
Well, life is full of disappointments. You need to toughen up. Don't let these things bother you.

Since Emily's parents have mastered the art of emotion coaching, they would address the situation differently:

Emily:
Mom, I'm so upset. My friend didn't invite me to her birthday party.

Parent:
Oh, Emily, that sounds really tough. I can see that it is making you sad. Do you want to talk about what happened?

Emily:
Yeah, Mom, I thought she was my friend, and I don't understand why she didn't invite me.

Parent:
It is okay to feel upset about this. Friendships can be complicated sometimes. How are you feeling right now?

Emily:
I just feel really left out.

Parent:
I understand, sweetie! Feeling left out can be really tough. If you are comfortable, we can talk about how you might handle this situation or what you want to do next.

And that is how Emily's parent opened a channel of honest communication with the child. Emotion coaching is all about approaching your kids through empathy and validating their emotions while guiding them along the way.

Emotion Coaching Through RULER Approach

One amazing approach to emotion coaching that was proposed by Jennings and Greenberg in 2009 is the RULER skills approach. According to this technique, there are five skills that can help parents connect with their children and help them learn emotional regulation. This technique is effective for people of all ages, young and adult which means that you can employ it yourself and let your kids learn from you:

- **R**ecognize

- **U**nderstand

- **L**abel

- **E**xpress

- **R**egulate

Once you help your kids learn this five-word formula they will never have to face difficulty dealing with their emotions. According to a research study published in 2019, students who experienced the RULER approach showed increased engagement and improved conduct while interacting with their classmates. Let's see how this approach works!

Recognize:
The first skill is to recognize the emotions. Whether it is reading other people's emotions or exploring our feelings, recognition is

the first milestone of this journey. You can teach kids to use body cues like posture, energy levels, and expressions to understand their own emotions and those of others. Let them create the connection between an emotion and how it is expressed.

Understand:
Understanding is the next part of this journey. Kids need to know that as humans we are allowed to feel all sorts of emotions. When they learn to identify the stimuli that lead to their uncomfortable feelings they can manage, anticipate, and prepare for an appropriate response.

Label:
There are more than 2,000 emotion words in the English language. Yet most of us have a very limited emotional vocabulary - that is why we fail to express our needs and desires appropriately. Our job is to help kids learn the language of emotions so they can speak through it effectively. Remember how we learned about the "emotion labeling" technique using the wheel of emotion in Chapter 2 of this book? Well, it's time to employ the same for your kids. You can create a wheel of emotions labeled according to the developmental phase of your child. For instance, for a 4-year-old, a wheel can only have basic emotions labeled such as happy, angry, sad, frustrated, fear, etc. You can continue adding more labels to the wheel as the child grows.

Express:
Expression is the linchpin of this process. The emotional vocabulary we learn and use to label the emotions helps us express ourselves better. At different times and in different contexts, some forms of expression are more effective than others. We need to teach our kids the different ways to express their emotions after assessing the situation. You can explain to children what you are doing and why, to provide them with models of different strategies to express their own emotions.

Regulate:
In this step, we must be able to ask ourselves, "*What can I do to maintain my feelings (if I want to continue feeling this way) or shift my feelings (if I do not want to continue feeling this way)?*" Ultimately, the goal of enhancing the emotional intelligence of children is to equip them with the tools and strategies to regulate what they feel. You can ask them to practice simple techniques like:

- **Belly Breathing:** For this, ask your child to place one hand on their chest and the other on their belly. Then tell them to inhale deeply through the nose, while feeling the belly rise. Now ask them to exhale slowly through the mouth. This activity helps activate the calming part of their nervous system.

- **Mindful Coloring:** You can provide coloring sheets and ask the child to focus on filling the pages with colors of their liking. This activity enhances concentration and can be a calming and creative outlet for expressing emotions.

- **Sensory Activities:** Activities like playing with playdough, kinetic sand, or using a stress ball can provide a constructive outlet for children to express their emotions.

- **Count to Ten:** Ask your child to count to ten slowly whenever they feel overwhelmed. This simple exercise helps redirect their attention and provides them with a pause before reacting impulsively.

- **Create a Calm-Down Corner:** Create a specific area in the home as a calm-down corner. Fill it with cozy cushions, sensory items, or a warm blanket. When your child feels upset, they can retreat to this space to self-regulate.

- **Journaling:** Giving a journal to your child to express emotion is one of the most effective techniques you can employ. You can ask them to draw colorful pictures, write stories, or write something they are grateful for to focus on the positive aspects of their day.

- **Guided Imagery:** Children are quite good with their imagination, so helping them to release stress through short visualizations and guided imagery can really help them regulate their emotions. In this exercise, you can ask them to close their eyes and imagine their happy place, this will significantly reduce their stress and anxiety.

Strategies for Effective Communication with Children

"Parents who are capable of expressing and regulating their emotions raise children who are more emotionally intelligent."
- Dr. Gottman

When it comes to dealing with children, effective communication is key. It is not just about what we say but how we say it. When your little ones are upset about something, instead of brushing it off or downplaying their emotions, try using words that acknowledge their feelings. For example, if they didn't get a toy they wanted, you could say, *"I get it, you really wanted that toy. It is totally okay to feel disappointed. Let's figure out what we can do together."* Effective communication is a powerful tool for imparting emotional intelligence to children. Here are some strategies to foster emotional intelligence through communication:

Resort to Active Listening:
You need to actively listen to children when they show the need to express themselves. When you put down your phone or stop whatever you are doing to listen to what they are sharing, you convey the message that their thoughts and emotions matter to you. Then you can repeat or paraphrase the things they say to give them a powerful confirmation that you not only heard their words but also comprehended the underlying feelings. This reflective listening process gives you a deeper understanding of their perspective and also reassures your child that their sentiments are not only acknowledged but genuinely valued. You can say things like, *"I hear you saying that you are frustrated because your friend didn't share the toy with you. Is that right?"* In this attentive and emotion-validating approach, you are creating a sense of emotional security, affirming that their voice is heard and their emotions are respected within the parent-child relationship.

Communicate Through Open-Ended Questions:
Open-ended questions create room for dialogue, and they allow the child to articulate their thoughts and feelings. It invites them to share their perspective and engage in meaningful conversations, promoting a deeper understanding of their inner world. This approach not only enhances their communication

skills but also demonstrates your genuine interest in their thoughts and emotions, reinforcing a sense of trust and openness in your parent-child relationship. You could say, *"How did that situation make you feel? Can you tell me more about it?"* This question will let your child know that you are genuinely interested in knowing the details of their problems.

Exercise Emotion Labeling:
It is pivotal to guide your child in identifying and labeling their emotions. When you encourage them to recognize and name their feelings, you are providing them with a crucial skill set to navigate their emotional landscape. This process not only helps them understand themselves better but also equips them to communicate their emotions more effectively. To further enhance their emotional vocabulary, engaging in interactive exercises can be beneficial.

For instance, you can play emotion charades where they act out different emotions or use emotion cards with various facial expressions and ask them to identify and discuss each feeling. These activities make the process of emotional labeling enjoyable and educational.

Offer Empathy and Validation:
When you show empathy and validation towards your child's feelings, you give them the ability to reciprocate that behavior. What all parents have to learn is that even when their perspective differs from that of their child, they have to show empathy and understanding. Immediately dismissing the ideas put out by a child is damaging behavior. Children see things from their evolving perspective, and we should give them the space to think freely without judgment. What we can do is offer them support, comfort, and suggestions without any judgment. When you show empathy by expressing understanding and support, it reinforces the idea that their feelings are valid and valued. For instance, if they are upset, then you can say something like, *"I can see this situation is really upsetting for you. It is okay to feel that way, and I'm here for you."* This approach cultivates trust, allowing your child to confide in you without fear of judgment, ultimately contributing to their emotional well-being and the development of healthy interpersonal skills.

Indulge in Problem-Solving Together:
To teach your children how to solve various problems, you

need to indulge them in finding solutions to different real-life challenges. Through this approach, you not only empower them to actively engage in resolving issues but also teach valuable skills for navigating life's complexities. This collaborative approach focuses on teamwork, communication, and critical thinking. You can also guide them in the process of thinking through problems and making decisions to instill a sense of autonomy and responsibility.

As they participate in decision-making, they develop problem-solving skills and gain confidence in their ability to tackle challenges. This not only strengthens the parent-child bond but also equips them with essential life skills, contributing to their emotional growth and resilience in the face of various situations. You can present a problem to them and then ask, *"What do you think we can do to make the situation better or prevent it from happening again?"* Another fun and educational problem-solving activity for children between the ages of 4-8 is creating a "Problem-Solving Box." Here's how you can set it up:

Materials Needed:
- A shoebox or any small box
- Colored markers, stickers, or craft supplies
- Index cards or small pieces of paper
- Writing instruments

You can decorate the box with colors, stickers, and any creative elements with your child. This makes the activity visually engaging and exciting. Then explain to your child that this box is their special place for solving problems and making decisions. It is a tool they can use whenever they come across a challenge. Together you can write down different challenges or problems that your child might face. These can range from school-related problems to friendship concerns or even scenarios they make up.

For each problem written down, ask your child to brainstorm possible solutions. Write these solutions on the back of the corresponding card. Allow your child to decorate the back of each card with positive and motivating elements. Then, whenever your child faces a challenge, have them pick a card from the box. Discuss the problem and explore the suggested solutions together. This activity is highly effective in promoting critical thinking and decision-making skills.

Model Behaviors and Emotions:
By modeling healthy emotional expression, you teach children about handling their own feelings. When you, as a parent, openly express your emotions in an appropriate manner, you show the importance of acknowledging and dealing with feelings constructively. Whether you are happy, frustrated, or stressed, let your children see that it is okay to experience a wide range of emotions as it helps normalize the human experience. For instance, after a rough day at work, you can say something like, *"I had a tough day at work today, and I'm feeling a bit stressed. I'm going to take a few minutes to relax and then we can play/chat."* By doing so, you create a safe environment where they learn not only to identify their emotions but also that expressing them is a natural and acceptable part of life. This modeling of emotional openness fosters a culture of understanding, empathy, and resilience within the family, laying the groundwork for your children to navigate their emotions with confidence and maturity.

Use Storytelling to Explore Emotions:
You know what they say, "Storytelling is the oldest form of education." It is also one of the effective methods to help children explore the world of emotions. With inspiring stories, they get to know all sorts of feelings and start feeling what others might be going through. After reading the stories, you can discuss the characters' emotions and the outcomes of their actions to enhance the child's understanding of cause and effect in emotional situations. For instance, if a character in a story expresses love or kindness, discuss how it positively affects others. This interactive approach not only broadens their emotional vocabulary but also encourages them to reflect on the impact of emotions and actions in real-life scenarios, contributing to their emotional development and social understanding.

Promote Reflection:
When you are talking about the consequences of their actions, keep it positive and judgment-free. Instead of just going on about what went wrong, help them think about other choices and the good stuff that could happen. For instance, if they had a disagreement with a friend, discuss not only what went wrong but also how they might approach similar situations differently in the future. This reflective process helps children build self-awareness, take responsibility for their actions, and develop the skills needed for constructive decision-making and

emotional regulation. It establishes a foundation for learning from experiences and making informed choices in various aspects of their lives.

Safe Space for Sharing:
When you are all about honesty, it signals to your child that sharing their thoughts and feelings is not just cool but important. Remind them that whatever they are feeling is totally okay; there's no right or wrong when it comes to emotions. You can assure them that their feelings are valid to reinforce the idea that there are no right or wrong emotions; all feelings are acceptable and part of being human. You can say things like, "*You can always talk to me about your feelings. I am here to listen and support you, no matter what.*" A supportive atmosphere provides a safe haven for your child to navigate and articulate their emotions. It helps them develop a healthy sense of self and the confidence to communicate with others.

Chapter 9

THE RIPPLE EFFECT

Your Children's Influences

Children are like sponges, they soak up everything they see. If we model negative behaviors, they are likely to pick up on that. But on the flip side, when we showcase positive behaviors, they learn that too. The responsibility of molding their minds and shaping their emotional intelligence heavily relies on us. It doesn't matter if our own childhood was marked by negative influence; we still have the chance to rewrite the script and do things differently for our kids. By making conscious changes in our behaviors, and practicing healthy habits, we can raise confident, secure, and emotionally intelligent children.

And it is not just about how we deal and communicate with our kids. A lot of things that children learn or mimic are the actions they observe. They are sensitive and highly perceptive, so even when we think that they are not listening, they are absorbing. They pick up vibes and sense the atmosphere around them. So, when parents indulge in the blame game during their disagreements (big or small), kids learn to not take responsibility for their actions. Similarly, when parents resort to aggression while communicating with their partner, kids pick that up too and likely re-enact that behavior during adulthood. Long story short - The kind of relationship you have with your partner is going to deeply influence the minds of your little ones.

A group of researchers who studied families in Nepal found

something interesting about how love between parents affects their children. They asked participants about how much they love each other. The parents could say "very much," "some," "a little," or "not at all." Then, they followed these parents' kids for 12 years to see what happened in their lives.

And guess what they found out? The children whose parents said they loved each other "some" or "very much" did better than the others in most areas of their lives. They stayed in school for a longer time, and they got married later. Now, why might this be happening? The researchers concluded that when parents love each other, they do more for their kids. They invest more time and effort in their children. Also, when parents love each other, the home environment is peaceful and happier. Happy homes might make kids less likely to hurry into their marriages. The researchers also thought that kids might see their parents as good examples. So, children take more time to find similar loving relationships when they grow up. This is how profound the impact of our relationship can be on the minds of our children.

Modeling Healthy Relationships: The Long-Term Effects

As we have established, children are excellent observers; they tend to learn more from what they see than what they are told. When we model healthy relationships that are loaded with love, expressed through respect and effective communication, our children learn that as norms for their future relationships. There was another study, conducted by the University of Virginia, and it found that *"the quality of a parent's relationship with each other plays a significant role in determining a child's future social skills."* Our role is not to create an unrealistic world where conflicts don't exist, but it is all about showing them how to deal with conflicts healthily. That is only possible when we become completely self-aware, equip ourselves with the healthy practices of conflict resolution, and practice open communication.

The Role of Affection

"Respond to your children with love in:

their worst moments
their broken moments
their angry moments
their selfish moments...
...it is in their most unlovable human moments that they need to feel loved." -L.R. Knost

Perhaps the role of affection in raising happy and secure children can never be overstated. Though we all love our kids unconditionally, when we don't invest enough time in expressing those emotions through warm hugs and words, children grow up learning to pent up their emotions and run away from them. This can lead to depression, anxiety, and complications in their future relationships. Whereas when children see their parents showing warmth and love openly, they mimic the same in their lives and embrace their emotions with confidence.

A study conducted by the University of Notre Dame in 2015, focused on the long-term effects of parental affection on children. About 600 individuals were surveyed to record their childhood experiences, including the amount of physical affection they received from their parents. Those people who reported higher levels of affection during childhood exhibited lower levels of depression and anxiety in adulthood and demonstrated greater compassion. In contrast, people who reported less affection in childhood struggled more with mental health, experienced heightened distress in social situations, and had difficulties relating to others' perspectives. So, as Dr. Gottman has already pointed out, *"Empathy not only matters; it is the foundation of effective parenting."* We need to deal with them with empathy, and affection to help them learn positive coping mechanisms.

How to Model Healthy Relationships?

"The Golden Rule of Parenting is do unto your children as you wish your parents had done unto you!" –Louise Hart

Was there something that you wanted your parents to do for you when you were little? Did you crave their affection or attention? Or did you have an amazing childhood, and you admire your parents for providing you with warmth and comfort to grow? Whatever it is that you think your parents could have done or did, take notes! Those are the things that you need to work on. For instance, if, as a child, you never had the space to talk openly about feelings, so make sure to create a non-judgmental atmosphere for your kids to speak up. There are several other things that you can do for them to pick up healthy ways to deal with relationships!

Emphasize Equality

The dominance of one parent over another creates a serious conflict in the minds of children. They have to see both parents working as a team on equal footing, otherwise, because of this imbalance they would naturally start seeing either of the genders as being weak. That distorts their perception of their own identity which could seriously disrupt their confidence. So, show them that equality is a virtue around the house and split every responsibility equally. Talk about it, and let the kids see that you make decisions mutually. Discuss finances, home chores, and other aspects of house management in front of them and let them see the power of collaboration.

Honest Communication

When kids see parents sharing their feelings openly, they do the same. For this to happen they need to be raised in a judgment-free atmosphere. So be honest when you talk, even when it is the tough stuff. Show them that is fine to talk about anything and listen when your partner shares. When you make a mistake, admit it, own it, and apologize, as it shows them that it is natural to mess up. The bottom line is to keep it real, keep it honest, and keep the talks open.

Demonstrate Self-Worth

Through the dynamics of your relationship, you can also show them to stand for self-worth. Yes, you are a team and you run the house together. But your individuality must also shine so your children can learn how to value their worth as individuals. Let them see this by celebrating your wins and failures in front of them. Share your interests and passions with them. You need to dedicate a small amount of time every day for yourself and do anything that you like - this will send a clear message to them about the value of self-worth.

Encourage Independence

Whether it is picking weekend activities, meal plans, or movie night choices, let them see that each voice in the house matters. Your actions can say to them, "You've got the power to make your own choices, and we're here to support you along the way." You can create an atmosphere of freedom by supporting your partner in pursuing their interests and passions, making it clear that everyone has the freedom to chase their dreams. Discuss all the decisions openly and let them see that choices come with responsibilities and consequences. When they observe you, both making choices and respecting each other's decisions, it sets the stage for them to embrace their autonomy responsibly.

Teach Accountability

When parents sow the seeds of accountability in their children, they hardly ever have to worry about punishing them for their wrongdoings. Through accountability, they learn to own their mistakes and try not to repeat them because they are aware of the harmful consequences, not because of the fear of punishment. To show them the ropes, own your actions, plain and simple. Let them witness that apologizing is a sign of respect and maturity. When you say you are going to do something, follow through. It shows reliability, and that is gold for them.

Model Healthy Conflict Resolution

Remember how we discussed effective conflict resolution techniques in previous chapters, it's about time to let the kids see the power of those methods. When disagreements arise, talk it out calmly without pointing fingers. They need to know that conflicts are a normal part of life, but they can be worked through with communication. If things get heated, it is cool to take a breather and come back to it later - let them see the effectiveness of stepping back to gain perspective. Listen up when your partner talks and let them see compromise in action. Allow your conflicts to be a lesson in communication, respect, and finding common ground. They will pick up some solid skills for handling bumps in the road.

Breaking Negative Family Patterns

"Emotionally intelligent families are more likely to create children who are socially able and show advanced 'prosocial' behavior." - Dr. John Gottman

There is no single definition of "negative family patterns." But you can identify them in common behaviors such as poor communication, abuse or neglect, controlling behavior, conditional love, lack of boundaries, perfectionism, emotional abuse, criticism, lack of empathy and the list goes on. Those behaviors become a pattern when each individual in the family fails to recognize the damage they can cause and does not actively work to avoid repeating them in their own lives. Luckily, those who have explored the power of emotional intelligence and self-awareness instantly recognize those patterns and try to break them so that the coming generations won't have to bear the brunt of them.

For instance, in Faith's family, perfectionism is a trait that appears to run in their blood. She had seen her grandmother criticizing every member of the family for not fluffing the cushions correctly to not tying shoelaces right. Some of her excessive criticism behavior traits were passed on to Faith's mom. While growing up, she couldn't understand why her mom acted the way she did. But after developing a deeper understanding of self and others, she began to understand that it was the ideal of "perfectionism" that made them do that. Faith herself also grew up to be a hyper-critical individual but then she read that *"perfectionism is the most paralyzing form of self-abuse."* This made her rethink things. She realized that being imperfect is what makes us human, and after years of self-exploration and struggle, she let go of the illusion of perfection. Life seems much more peaceful and happier since then!

All it takes is one realization to change it all. We can break the patterns and let our children grow in an open and positive atmosphere where they can make mistakes, learn from them, and embrace their true selves. According to a study published in the Journal of Family Psychology, it was concluded that children raised in emotionally responsive environments are more likely to develop secure attachment styles and better emotional regulation skills. So, if your family lacks an emotionally responsive environment, we need to change that starting from now.

Breaking the Patterns:
"Consider letting go of the barriers between yourself and others, let go of the definition our culture has inflicted upon us, and allow the best part of ourselves to connect with the wondrous parts of others." - David W. Earle

Breaking family patterns can be like trying to change the course of a river; they have been flowing for so long that they become deeply ingrained in our minds. It is not just a challenge from the outside but also a battle within. It feels comfortable to follow something familiar no matter how toxic it is, as disrupting that comfort can stir up resistance. However, when we stop to realize the potential harm these patterns may be causing, not just to us but also to the coming generation, motivation kicks in. It is this awareness that acts as a compass to guide us down the road of breaking those patterns.

Self-Reflection and Awareness:
Speaking of awareness, one tool that is going to help you a lot during this whole journey is self-reflection! Since we deeply delved into self-awareness in the first chapter of this book, I am not going to repeat the techniques and methods to explore ourselves, but I would like to take a moment here to highlight its importance in breaking negative family patterns. I have seen people blindly following family norms, not questioning themselves or others for their actions. That is because they never take the time to reflect and see beneath the surface. It is important to diagnose the problem before we begin to solve it, and that's what self-awareness helps us do.

Understand the Origin:
Why is it important to know the origin of a pattern? To question its validity! If there is something you notice in your behavior, you should ask yourself, *"Where is this coming from?"*

When you identify the origin of a pattern, you get to learn its outcomes by looking at the lives of the people who have been following it. Since Faith saw her mother beating herself up all the time for not meeting her own expectations, her anger and frustration, Faith realized the outcomes of following the same pattern all over again. So, whatever troubling behavior you recognize in yourself, in your partner, or anyone else, look for the origin of that pattern and it will tell you exactly what you should not be doing!

Acceptance and Ownership:
Without accepting the problem, you cannot eradicate it. You need to realize that no family is perfect, and we all need to change certain things to grow healthy patterns of behavior. So, follow the idea of taking ownership of your role in perpetuating these patterns. The next generation is counting on your personal evolution and recognizes that your contribution is pivotal to initiating positive change.

Communication and Open Dialogue:
Without open communication and dialogue, we cannot effectively break negative patterns. Whether it's you or your partner who has some troubling behaviors that you don't want your kids to learn from you, you will have to talk about it. So, create an environment where your family members can feel encouraged to express their thoughts and feelings without fear of judgment. Even if you think that your parents made a mistake while raising you, talk to them about it! You will get to learn things from their perspective, and it will help you do things differently and avoid those same mistakes. Instead of avoiding challenging conversations, establish a safe space where family members can openly share their perspectives and concerns.

Establishing Boundaries:
It is imperative to clearly define personal space and respect the boundaries of every individual in the family. Whether it is your partner, your kids, or anyone in the house, they have the right to spend time with themselves and explore their inner voice, interests, and passions. When we introduce personal boundaries, it suffocates people and often leads them to shut us out completely. So, it is best to establish healthy boundaries.

Positive Reinforcement:
Another way to break negative patterns is to gradually introduce positive reinforcement. It is a powerful tool in shaping family dynamics. Through this method, you highlight and appreciate constructive actions taken by the family member. For instance, if your kids help you with the house chores, then appreciate their efforts. With active acknowledgment, cooperation, and support, we create a positive atmosphere.

Practice Positive Behavior:

To get rid of the old habits, we need to switch to new ones. The more you consciously practice positive behaviors like displaying empathy in your interactions with family members, the more they become part of your personality genome. And once you start practicing them, kids pick them up automatically. Initially, you might face some internal resistance, but in just a matter of months, you will see change within yourself and others around you.

However, you should understand that change takes time, and it is a gradual process. Breaking negative patterns is a slow and long-term journey, so be kind to yourself in this process and continue celebrating your wins while looking forward.

PART V

Creating Lasting Happiness through Emotional Connection

Chapter 10

EVERYDAY CONNECTION

Keeping the Spark Alive

The fantasy of having that "perfect moment" has made many of us lose valuable time in our lives. We are so obsessed with looking for "special" moments, days, or celebrations that we often overlook the beauty of the ordinary and the mundane. One of the key elements to lasting happiness in a relationship is the consistent emotional connection, the little things we do for each other on a daily basis. A study published in the Journal of Social and Personal Relationships found that couples who keep their emotional connection alive by doing small, everyday things together experience greater satisfaction and longevity in their relationships. So, it is not just about grand gestures or expensive gifts; it is the little things that count. Small acts like making a cup of coffee for your partner in the morning, asking about their day, or giving them a hug when they come home can have a profound impact on your relationship's health and happiness. If you want to keep the spark alive in your relationship, remember that everyday connections matter more than you might think.

Small Gestures Matter

"It is the small, positive moments in our relationships that have the most lasting impact." - John Gottman

Have you ever heard the saying, *"It is the little things that count"*? When it comes to relationships, it couldn't be truer. Expressing our love and care towards our partner is a fundamental aspect of a healthy relationship. Imagine if you surprise your partner with their favorite snack or a cup of tea. These small acts shout, "I love you" louder than words. I call small gestures the stabilizers of a relationship. When you consistently show your partner that they matter through these thoughtful acts, it creates a sense of security. It is your way of saying, *"You are important to me, and I am here for you."* This reduces uncertainty and strengthens the bond you share.

The value of these gestures goes beyond just material gifts. There was this survey conducted with over 5,000 participants and it revealed something worth mentioning here. According to its results, it was found that it was not the material gifts like flowers or chocolates that stole the show; it was the thoughtfulness behind the gesture.

Even a simple *"I love you"* is not just three words; it is a powerful affirmation. It reassures your partner that your feelings are strong and unwavering. In a world filled with uncertainties, knowing you're loved is like a warm embrace. It brings couples closer and strengthens their emotional connection. Such expression of love is not just good for the heart; it is good for mental health too. A study in 2020 found that experiencing love on a daily basis had remarkable effects. It elevates self-esteem, gives a sense of purpose, increases our optimism, and contributes to an overall sense of well-being. Those small gestures contribute to this daily dose of love, making both partners feel emotionally fulfilled and supported.

What Gestures?

"In love, small gestures matter just as much as the big ones. They are the daily affirmations of your affection." - Esther Perel

I know what must be going through your mind right now! It's the possible list of "small gestures" that you can put to use, isn't it? Well, if you are scratching your head for ideas, then let me share some powerful gestures that any couple can use, and they work like magic.

Vocalize Your Affection:
They say action speaks louder than words. But sometimes, hearing those words is also good for the mind and mood. So, verbal expression is also important. Here is how you can do it:

- Say it out loud: Make saying "*I love you*" a regular habit. It is a simple phrase, but it holds immense power.

- Compliment them: Tell your partner they look good. Acknowledge the effort they put into their appearance.

- Share laughter: Find joy in shared jokes. Listening to them and laughing at their jokes is also a great gesture.

- Text messages: Try to send them sweet text messages to surprise them. A simple "*thinking of you*" goes a long way.

- Phone calls: Call them just to hear their voice. It shows you are thinking of them.

- Express gratitude: Tell them that you are thankful for both big and small things they do for you.

- Personalized compliments: Give unique compliments tailored to your partner. It shows you see and appreciate their individuality.

- Express your luck: Let them know how lucky you feel to have them in your life. It is a beautiful affirmation.

- Express missing them: When apart, communicate that you miss them. It keeps the emotional connection strong.

Create Intimacy:
Enough with the words! Let's explore the physical gestures that you can use to create intimacy and strengthen your bond!

- Try to hold hands with your partner more often and give hugs and kisses for no reason.

- Keep them close to you when either of you is upset and provide comfort and support.

- Reach out to your partner first thing in the morning instead of your phone.

- Go for frequent touches, whether a shoulder squeeze or a hand on their back. Physical connection matters.

- Explore new ways to be intimate with each other. It keeps the relationship spark.

Acts of Service:
We all have our love languages. If your partner's love language is an act of service, then go with gestures like:

- Cooking meals for them to show you care.

- Surprising them with breakfast in bed. It is a gesture of pampering.

- Taking care of them when they are unwell. Small acts of service during illness speak volumes.

- Helping them with chores, finishing their tasks, and supporting them.

- Staying quiet when they are sleeping. It shows consideration for their needs.

- Helping them with errands. It is a practical way to show support.

- Being mindful of their preferences and boundaries. Respect their personal space.

- Looking for ways to help them with things they find challenging.

- Showing real effort in improving your own bad habits. It reflects a commitment to personal growth.

Surprise Them With a Gift:
Lastly, it comes to material surprises! They don't have to be big and expensive; you can even try smaller thoughtful gifts like:

- Sweet handwritten notes.

- Fresh flowers from the garden. It is a natural and thoughtful gift.

- Mints on their pillow.

- Take them shopping to get them things they want.

Besides those gifts, you can buy things based on their tastes and interests. It shows you pay attention. Also, show appreciation for the gifts they give you. And don't forget important occasions. It reflects attentiveness and care.

Establishing Rituals as a Couple

Relationship rituals are like the secret sauce of love, sprinkled over the routine to make it extra special. One relationship ritual can be meeting your partner after work on Mondays, not just to see them but to cheer each other up. It can turn an ordinary day into a celebration, a day uniquely owned by the dynamic duo. Sure, there are the classics like birthdays and anniversaries, but you can create your own rituals as well. Rituals are your backstage pass to your exclusive show, away from the family circus. And I am talking about spiritual rituals too - because why not? Nothing says 'togetherness' like synchronized meditation.

So, whether it is a simple Monday pick-me-up or a spiritual two-step during the holidays, these relationship rituals are the love glue. They turn the mundane into the extraordinary and give couples a shared history that's as unique as they are, a history written in inside jokes, shared smiles, and the occasional Friday victory dance. Here are some interesting relationship rituals that you can add to your daily lives:

- Pillow Talk: An intimate conversation during waking or bedtime, sharing hopes, dreams, and vulnerabilities is a great way to end or start your day

- No Digital Time: You can designate a time free from electronic distractions to focus on each other.

- Consistent Bedtime: Try to go to bed at the same time each day. Going to bed together will enhance connection and intimacy.

- Fitness Together: You can pick up a few exercises that you can do together, like morning walks, yoga, or cycling, etc.

- First-Person News: When you share personal news with your partner first, it creates a sense of immediate connection.

- Evening Greetings: It is another healthy ritual you can incorporate. Give your partner a warm and enthusiastic greeting when reuniting after some time apart.

- Serious Discussions: For serious discussions or to resolve conflicts, it is best to allocate specific time so you can listen to each other more actively.

Now you can create your own unique rituals as per your needs and desires by discussing them with your partner. Whatever you do, do not skip them because those rituals are the daily affirmations of love that keep your spark alive.

Patience - the Road to Wisdom

Love always demands patience! No relationship is perfect, and it takes time to understand your partner and to grow together as a couple. If a relationship is a garden, then patience is like sunlight and water that nurtures it. It gives your love room to breathe and makes your communication smoother.

How to Have Patience in a Relationship

We are living in the age of quick results. We need to see change happening fast. But nothing evolves overnight. Relationships are difficult, you are going to have arguments, debates, and discussions about your differences. But remember, if there is love, you two can make it work with patience. All those techniques and strategies we have learned so far, take time to bring results. Relationships are not fast food, so take time to understand and grow with your partner. Slow down; it is not a race. You just have to continuously nurture your relationship with the power of empathy and understanding. Now, there will be times when you might lose your cool! But here is how you can get through them:

- Give up the need to be right. Living with a partner is all about finding a middle ground. Proving yourself right isn't going to get you a medal, so go for a win-win solution.

- Before reacting to a situation, count to three. It gives space for patience and reason to kick in.

- Unrealistic expectations keep you disappointed all the time. Don't set expectations too high. Be realistic. Patience is easier when you know what to expect.

- Your partner is beautifully human, with flaws and all. Accept them for who they are and not for what they could have been.

- Lastly, keep yourself physically and mentally fit through exercise. It is easier to practice patience when you are strong.

Path to Mutual Understanding & Respect

So far, we have learned various effective exercises to improve communication, develop understanding, and resolve conflicts with our partners. Most of those strategies including the art of reflective listening, journaling together, mindfulness, and meditation are going to be extremely helpful in allowing you to understand your partner and respect them for who they are. However, there are other exercises as well that will help boost your mutual understanding:

Empathy Mapping

I am borrowing this idea from the field of UI/UX designing, but I find it extremely helpful in understanding partners as well. Empathy mapping is a technique in which before designing the user interface of a website or an application, the designer draws a map to put themselves in the user's shoes and understand their needs and desires. You and your partner can do the same! Draw a circle and divide it into sections representing different areas of your life. Discuss and map out each other's current emotional state in these areas. This exercise can help you visualize each other's emotional landscapes and areas that may need attention.

Question Cards

Another interesting way to learn about each other's emotional state is to do a quick quiz. Think of it as a fun game. You can write questions or use existing questionnaires from the internet to ask your partner about their deeper feelings, values, and thoughts. In this way, you won't only get to know them better, but you will also strengthen your bond by sharing this fun time.

Role Swap

This one is a fun exercise. It is a guessing game but for emotions. You can take turns guessing how your partner feels about a situation. It helps to understand how you two see each other and that leads to better understanding. You can then reflect on the emotions. Through this exercise, you end up clearing a lot of differences and misunderstandings in a fun way.

Chapter 11

VULNERABILITY AND INTIMACY

Deepening Your Love Connection

"The strongest love is the love that can demonstrate its fragility."
— Paulo Coelho, Eleven Minutes

Emotional vulnerability gives space to true intimacy. Unfortunately, many of us see vulnerability as a weakness and people fear sharing their shortcomings with their partners just to look strong and secure. While doing so, they mask their true selves and lose authenticity. Many fear that opening up about their insecurities would make their partner see them differently. It is the fear of criticism and judgment that builds a wall between two partners. However, both science and experience have proved that the more partners share their fears and dreams with one another, the stronger their relationship gets. Such a bond is built on trust, honesty, and truth instead of fake pretenses.

Demonstrating your fragility is difficult when you are raised in a society that tells you that showing emotion is a sign of weakness and we always have to keep it together. We naturally learn to develop these emotional barriers around us, to not let the world see and judge us for who we are. Before we begin this chapter, make a promise to present the authentic version of yourself to the world and let your partner, loved ones, friends and others see and accept who you are - the way you are!

Break Down Emotional Barriers

"Vulnerability is the birthplace of innovation, creativity and change." - Brene Brown

If you have ever had your heart broken or you were raised in an insecure or hostile environment as a child, then you must have built a fort around your inner self. The fear of emotional hurt is similar to any other phobias we carry. Just as the fear of heights keeps us from enjoying the best views in the world, the fear of re-experiencing past emotional traumas keeps us from exploring the warmth and comfort of an emotionally available partner.

You are so afraid of the hurt that the mere idea of letting anyone step into your emotional boundaries and mess with your feelings scares you. And that is how emotional barriers are built. It is a natural self-preserving coping mechanism that prevents you from experiencing any future hurt. You lower your expectations when it comes to dealing with people, you don't share your true feelings, and you avoid feeling too strongly which gradually leads to emotional numbness. When you build these walls around, you focus so deeply on preventing the sadness that you also miss out on experiencing the intense feeling of joy. You constantly doubt your partner, experience difficulty managing emotions, and do not seek healthy methods of conflict resolution. Invulnerability is a self-sabotaging act that disrupts the foundation of a healthy romantic relationship. If any of those signs sounds familiar to you then it's about time to break those walls and let your heart experience the warmth of intimacy and trust. Here are some impactful methods that you can try. But before I begin listing those strategies, I suggest you first find a suitable way to resolve your particular childhood traumas or negative past experiences, to open your heart and mind to new possibilities. This may include *Inner Child Healing* work, whether through self-help guides and books or a therapist experienced in this work.

To break those emotional barriers, you need to focus on the foundation. Explore the factors that made you create these walls in the first place. Recall your experiences and pinpoint the reasons. Was it because either of your parents was not available to meet your emotional needs? Did any of your loved ones abandon you or were you cheated on by someone? This will give you the right perspective. You can share your grievances, fears, and insecurities with your partner to gradually shake the walls down. If you face trouble sharing all the details, start with the smaller ones. But don't wait around to find the perfect time or moment, just sit down and talk.

Instead of focusing on the hurt, pay attention to how much you evolved. You learn and become the person you are today by going through those painful experiences. So, reframe your negative thoughts and let yourself believe that you can change your own story by letting your partner become part of your internal struggle.

While you work on your expression of vulnerability, keep in mind that it is a two-way street. You and your partner have to be equally vulnerable and open to each other to create room for a judgment-free atmosphere. There are ways in which you can help your partner bring down their emotional walls as well:

1. Constantly show your interest in them. People having difficulty sharing their emotions crave assurances, so your care, love, and show of affection will help in your partner's healing of past traumas.

2. Be an active listener and ask them how you can help. Such actions will help make them feel comforted, heard, and valued.

3. Let your partner see how much you value their presence in your life.

Lastly, don't push too hard! Finding comfort in being vulnerable is a difficult process and it often takes time to break down barriers built over many years. So, whether it is you or your partner dealing with emotional barriers, take the time and space necessary to heal.

Trust-Building Exercises

They say the best proof of love is trust. The trust between two partners provides a safe foundation, but life isn't always smooth sailing. Conflicts and differences between two partners can impact the level of trust they both have for each other. However, trust can be built, and rebuilt, by effectively being open and honest with each other and employing trust-building exercises.

Not only do these activities keep ignorance and distrust out of the picture, but they also bring partners closer to one another which paves the way to deeper intimacy. Let's explore some of the widely recommended techniques for trust-building!

Eye Gazing:

Eye gazing is one of the highly recommended tantric exercises. According to Hindu and Buddhist "tantra" philosophy which existed even 3,000-5,000 years ago, looking into your partner's eyes for an extended period strengthens your spiritual connection.

It also makes you and your partner feel more open and vulnerable. You can do this once or twice a week, 10-20 minutes at a time, to keep the connection strong. It sounds like such a simple exercise, but it can be enormously effective and build a stronger emotional connection between you.

Appreciation and Gratitude Ritual:

Develop the ritual of appreciating one another regularly. This exercise not only helps with trust but also enhances connection while breaking the emotional walls. Highlighting one quality of each other can create a positive environment which can also give space to vulnerability.

Blindfolded Obstacle Course:

This is a fun activity that you can even try with any of your couple-friends at a party or on a game night. For this, you create an obstacle course, which can be anywhere in your living room or your backyard. Spread tennis balls or any other objects around and blindfold one of the partners. Now the other partner has to guide the blindfolded partner with verbal instructions to find the balls/objects and grab them. This exercise enhances the ability to actively listen and trust one another.

Trust Fall:

This one is a classic trust exercise that you have probably seen people doing on television or in movies. In this activity, one partner has to fall backward while relying on the other to catch them from behind. Just make sure whichever of you is doing the catching is positioned to catch the 'faller' safely and securely. The act of falling and catching one another promotes trust in each other.

Share Stories & Communicate Openly:

Another way to enable trust is by sharing your personal stories, childhood memories, and special moments with your partner. When you share, it reflects your trust in them, and they would reciprocate the same by sharing about themselves. It doesn't have to be something huge, anything that you feel comfortable sharing can make a difference. Create a regular practice of communicating with one another at a time when there are no distractions around. A study conducted by the Sage Colleges also confirmed that "open communication about emotions leads to greater relationship satisfaction."

Mirror Exercise:

Here is another fun exercise! In this, you and your partner have to work in pairs. Either one of you can take the lead and the other one would have to mirror the movement of the leading partner. This exercise enhances trust and non-verbal communication.

Share Goals and Experiences

A sense of camaraderie and togetherness develops when you set similar goals and engage in shared activities together. As a couple, you can create a relationship vision board and add short-term and long-term targets to achieve. By indulging in this process that may involve brainstorming, working out solutions to your household or relationship problems, managing finances, and planning recreational activities together you can create an atmosphere of trust and openness. This way, you also learn to resolve your disagreements and concentrate on the collective good.

Creating Space for Emotional Dialogue

Focus on Family Singapore carried out a research study in which a statement was presented to participating couples: *"It is difficult to share my deepest thoughts and feelings with my spouse."* About 30 percent of the total respondents strongly agreed or agreed with this statement. The reason why people experience difficulty in sharing their feelings with their partners is their relationship hasn't created an open and healthy atmosphere for emotional dialogue. Feelings of defensiveness, distrust, or disconnect can hinder open communication, and you may feel anxious while opening up about your feelings. We don't deliberately let this happen! However, with deliberate efforts, we can recreate a space for open emotional dialogue. One of the effective formulas I recommend is "SAFER". It is an acronym for a combination of different strategies that you can employ:

Set - a Positive Tone

When you see your partner after a long day at work, what do you say to them? Do you complain, nag, or greet each other with a snide remark? If so, then this would set a negative tone for your conversation. No matter how bad your day was, while talking to your partner, your tone has to be positive. With so much negativity already going around, you both must be a source of relief from that, a haven of positive energy for one another. So, greet your partner with a positive tone, and include compliments and gestures of concern as a part of your relationship "care" routine. Being with each other is a soothing relief from the workday. Your tough day at work or a recent argument with the boss doesn't have to define your communication with your partner. Having said that, of course, you can share your day's challenges with your partner later. But the fact you came back together at the end of the working day in an uplifting and positive way sets the tone for the rest of the day.

A friend of mine once shared that every day while driving home from work he switches his mindset and reminds himself that his family deserves the best of his words and actions. So, whatever happens at the office, he leaves that in the car and only takes love and gracious words to his partner and kids. This created a reassuring and warmer atmosphere at his home which allowed him to have deeper dialogues with his spouse.

Avoid - An Absolute Language

Absolute language is the "kill bill" of open and honest communication. Such words may upset your partner or force them to keep their true feelings to themselves.

What is an absolute language? You might wonder! It includes sentences like:

"You always interrupt when I speak."

"You are always on your phone when I am talking to you."

"You never ask for my opinions regarding any issue."

It is a language in which you point the finger at your partner, making them defensive. Such language makes the partner on the receiving end withdraw from the conversation emotionally. So, make sure to avoid it. Instead of shifting the blame to them, just ask what is required in the situation. In this way, the same sentences given in the previous example can be replaced with:

"May I finish speaking before you share your opinion?"

"Would you mind putting the phone down and listen to me?"

"I would like you to consider my opinions and views on [this issue]."

Focus - on Listening Instead of Making Point

When you focus on making your point and proving yourself right, you miss the actual point. You and your partner are not in a fighting ring ready to win the next WWE championship - this is a relationship where it is you and your partner versus the world. If you keep fighting and proving your point you will fail to listen and understand each other. Even if you disagree with each other's views, carefully listen to one another first, avoid misunderstandings, and then sit together to come up with a solution that works for both of you. Instead of judging your partner, bring some curiosity into the picture. Ask them questions and try to understand why your partner holds certain beliefs and views. Learn to accept the differing views to create an open space for dialogue.

Emotions – Be Aware of Them

Emotions can make a conversation complex and set its tone. Sometimes, emotions can get high during a conversation, and if you choose to react spontaneously without thinking it may push your partner into a defensive mode or hurt their feelings. So, in such a situation go for a more gracious approach and take a moment before reacting. If your emotional reaction is triggered, ask yourself, "*Is it because of fear, embarrassment, or pride?*" There is no harm in hitting the pause button to first reflect and then pick up the conversation later when you are ready to deal with the situation objectively.

Respect - Each Other's Boundaries

Another factor that pushes a partner to withdraw emotionally from a relationship is the invasion of their boundaries. Everyone needs their personal space to thrive in, and sometimes you simply need the time to process emotions, thoughts, and feelings first before sharing with anyone - even the partner sitting next to you. Now, it is only fair to offer such space to your partner and let them feel free to express themselves whenever they are comfortable. Forceful confessions and expressions never work in favor of an authentic conversation and a healthy relationship. So, respect your partner's boundaries, and let them know that you are open to discussion and that you are there for them. But do not nag them for not sharing.

Eric Michael Leventhal once said, "*We are at our most powerful moment when we no longer need to be powerful,*" and it beautifully describes the power of vulnerability. As long as there is a loving and accepting partner sitting next to you, never fear to open up and share your feelings. Initially, it might feel like a challenge, but with the gradual incorporation of trust-building exercises and the creation of a safe space for dialogue, you two can foster a bond with lasting happiness.

Chapter 12

FUTURE-PROOFING YOUR LOVE STORY

A few years back, I read somewhere that "*a true relationship is two imperfect people refusing to give up on each other.*" I believe that is the secret of future-proofing your love story! When you are willing to make it work against all the odds and challenges, because the bond you share with your partner is something worth keeping and saving, you actively manage the difficulties as a team.

According to Linda Carroll, a relationship and family therapist, there are five stages of every relationship:

1. The first is the "merge", or the honeymoon phase as we all know it. During this phase, you see the other person as your perfect match. The mix of dopamine, oxytocin, and endorphins, fogs your brain so you ignore to see any incompatibilities.

2. But as soon as this phase ends, you enter into the denial and doubt phase where the unexplored issues and potential incompatibilities start surfacing.

3. When you reach the point where you start acknowledging the issues, you enter into the "disillusionment" phase, and you realize that the

relationship is not all about the happy moments.

4. Then comes the most difficult phase and you decide whether you would want to give up on each other just because it is difficult, or you want to preserve it because it makes you happy and contented. This is the breaking point.

5. When couples actively engage in healthy conflict resolution techniques, regulate their emotions, communicate, and stay truly vulnerable during this stage, they then step into the phase of "wholehearted love" which offers lasting peace and happiness. You might face several hiccups on this road, but with resilience, trust, and emotional intelligence you both can steer through them.

Some of the problems that you should look out for while navigating your relationship in the long run include:

Parenting Challenges:

The difference in parenting styles, the idea of discipline, and balancing the couple's dynamic can be another area of challenge. Remember the lessons in Chapters 8 and 9, and you will be on the way to resolving such problems.

Miscommunication:

Throughout the whole transition that we just learned about; a relationship experiences several blows. It may fall into the patterns of miscommunication especially when partners refuse to accept differences, look past them, and avoid confrontation due to the fear of potential conflict.

Intimacy and Romance:

Intimacy and romance may also hit the side curb when you both get distracted by daily stress, busy work schedules, and other life commitments.

Changing Priorities:

As individuals, you evolve and grow different priorities. Your career, lifestyle, and family planning choices change and that may cause a drift between you and your partner. Unless you two discuss and come to common ground on several life aspects, the changing priorities will remain a challenge.

Financial Stress:

Disagreements over money management and financial goals can be stressful and they can put a strain on a relationship. Debt, differing spending habits, or economic downturns can all cause differences.

Work-Life Balance:

When you constantly have to juggle career responsibilities with personal and family life, then this pressure may affect the quality of the relationship. To not let work-related stress affect your bond, you will have to draw a line to create some boundaries and leave work out of the personal space.

Routine and Monotony:

You know what they say, *"Monotony kills the substance,"* and that is what happens when we let a sense of boredom or dissatisfaction prevail in a relationship. You need to actively work to introduce variety, spontaneity, and shared experiences to keep the relationship dynamic and alive.

External Influences:

External factors like family dynamics, societal expectations, or cultural differences can also get in the way of a healthy relationship. You can beat them by staying true to your relationship values.

Lack of Individual Growth:

Sometimes when either one of the partners fails to grow as an individual, that may automatically create distance and difference between the couple.

The truth is that the key to lasting happiness in a long-term relationship is not avoiding issues and challenges, but looking those problems in the eye, holding your partner's hand, and navigating through them by putting your individual and collective emotional intelligence to use.

Managing Life Changes Together

"*Change is the constant*"- I bet you must have heard those wise words by Heraclitus! As poignant as that statement is, we cannot deny the inevitability of change. Life is no doubt full of highs and lows. So, no matter how strong your connection with your partner is, it is going to be tumultuous at some point and you both can ride those waves with success by managing those changes together.

Learn the Art of Communication

From creating deeper intimacy to resolving conflicts and expressing vulnerability, one act that remains crucial for a healthy relationship is "open communication." Time and again, throughout this book we have gone through many techniques to maintain effective communication with your partner. At the risk of sounding repetitive, I suggest you invest your time in learning the art of communication - trust me, this will help you with every interaction you will have in your life. Listen actively, process the emotions, and share what then comes to mind - these three steps form the basis of good communication. Having fears? Dealing with doubts? Just talk and let your partner in on what is going through your mind.

Invest Time:

As Dr. John Gottman once said, "*Emotionally intelligent couples are intimately familiar with each other's world.*" Familiarity and understanding develop by spending quality time with your partner. It is not just the expressed words that help you learn the deepest desires of one another but the shared experience of engaging in activities that you both love. If spending a great quantity of time together is neither feasible nor practical, focus on the quality of the time you do spend together. Whenever you get the chance to plan a special date together, go out, have fun, and let your inner child bloom as you spend time with your favorite person.

Nurture Emotional Connection:

Empathy, affection, and mutual respect are the three tenets of deep emotional connection. Offer them with consistency and you will have a connection that will bind your souls together. When things get tough, that is when empathy is most needed. Constantly put yourself in your partner's position to assess the situation and then discuss the problems to come to common terms.

Teamwork:

When life throws changes at you, deal with them as a team. Think of it as playing tennis together! When you both work together to identify common goals and make decisions, you will be at a greater advantage than dealing with problems alone. As a team, you both can work in the collective interest of your relationship. No matter how tough the situation gets, think of it as "you and your partner against the world." This will form a strong foundation for your relationship.

Maintain Individual Identities:

While being a team is necessary, it is also crucial to keep your identities alive. Dr. Terri Orbuch, a renowned psychologist, recommends maintaining individuality within the relationship. Losing your personal touch, and neglecting your interests and passion are not healthy for you and your relationship. You can only contribute well to your relationship by becoming the best version of yourself. So, it is wise to keep encouraging each other to pursue personal interests and goals. This makes sure that each person continues to grow and evolve within the relationship. While doing so, also dedicate some time for self-care, be it as an individual or as a couple. The health of your relationship lies in the emotional and physical well-being of you and your partner, so take care of yourselves.

Celebrate Achievements:

Striving through changes becomes much easier and more motivating when you both continue celebrating each achievement along the way. Continuously acknowledge and appreciate the efforts that you both put into managing life changes. This positive reinforcement strengthens the bond between you both.

Keep the Spark Alive: Love Languages and Beyond

Most couples fear that their chemistry will fade with time and that often becomes the case when long-term relationships are left stagnant. When the relationship enters into the last phase of "wholehearted love" (mentioned at the beginning of this chapter), couples assume that from that point forward things will remain the same. However, the steadier the flow of the relationship gets, the more attention it requires to keep things exciting and alive. If you also share the same concerns and want to keep the fire of intimacy burning, then here are some easy-to-do, everyday activities that will help.

Greet Your Partner

Find an affectionate way to greet your partner every time you see them after time away, even if it's after being at work. Whether it is a kiss, a hug, or anything that would rekindle the warmth you two share. Showing your partner affection, telling them that they were missed keeps the relationship thriving.

Appreciate Them

"The deepest principle in human nature is the craving to be appreciated." — William Jones

Even though you may have told your partner a million times before how much you appreciate them, use every day as an opportunity to express your love and gratitude, and show this through verbal praise.

It always feels good to hear someone you love appreciating you.

Unplug From the World

"You are always looking at your mobile screen whenever I talk to you." This is one of the most common arguments that couples have these days. You can't engage in self-reflection, active listening, and emotional dialogue when you are constantly distracted by your mobile phone "pinging" in the middle of the conversation. So, disconnect from the world for a while, and keep your phones aside, especially when you plan to spend quality time together. Be mindful when talking to your partner and engaging with them.

Leave Love Notes

If you don't get the chance to talk to your partner before leaving home for work or before getting to sleep, then leave little love notes for them to read whenever they get the chance. Notes are daily reminders that you miss one another and despite the busy schedule, you are thinking about them. Alternatively, you can send them compassionate texts now and then. Add an element of surprise to give each other a sudden boost of excitement.

Try New Activities Together

Repeating the same old love rituals can make your relationship really boring and stale. If you want to keep it exciting, then step out of your comfort zone and engage in adventurous activities together. You can even learn new skills together to strengthen your bond and experience personal growth as well.

Make Time for Date Night

Don't miss out on the date nights. Dating fuels connection and it keeps the relationship from going stagnant. When you disconnect from the rest of the world, it enables you and your partner to keep the connection growing.

Take Time to Miss Them

Personal time is not just important for self-care, but it is also crucial to keep enough space from your partner to let them miss you. When you are always around each other, it could lead to taking for granted or, worse, indifference, which is the death of a relationship. Craving for your partner for a certain period of time can ignite passion and always keep you two on the edge. Plan a vacation with your friends or family and take time for yourself to let your partner miss you. A little distance makes the heart grow fonder.

The bottom line is that healthy, and meaningful relationships grow when they are nurtured. Whether you have been together for 4 months, 4 years, or 40 years, keeping that spark alive is important to strengthen the relationship. Continue doing what you two did back in the early days of your relationship, so the fire won't fizzle out. Your connection will constantly flourish if you care for it with commitment.

CONCLUSION

Before wrapping up this book, I would like to congratulate you for taking the first step toward building a deeper and healthier relationship. This book has encapsulated the whole idea of exploring relationship potential through the power of emotional intelligence. I trust that each chapter in this book has proven a valuable resource to you.

Now the work begins!

We have delved deeply into proven and successful emotional intelligence-boosting strategies, giving you 10 steps for your relationship blueprint, which include a number of strategies, techniques and exercises:

1. Discover your hidden self

2. Emotional balance

3. Core values

4. Empathy

5. Communication skills

6. Conflict management and graceful disagreement

7. Building trust

8. Keeping the spark alive

9. Vulnerability and intimacy

10. Future-proofing your love story

Together, we started by learning the depth of emotional intelligence, its role and significance in our lives, and then dove headfirst into the components of EI - self-awareness, emotional regulation, motivation, empathy, and social skills.

After looking deeply into the emotional intelligence components, we turned to the healthy conflict resolution techniques which were followed by post-conflict healing strategies.

Not only did we discuss the use of EI to strengthen the relationship between partners, but we also learned about using the power of this awareness to raise happy, secure, and emotionally intelligent kids.

We discovered the secrets to fostering lasting happiness while embracing the power of vulnerability. Lastly, we delved into the methods of future-proofing the bond to navigate through the challenges of life as a couple and as an individual.

Don't forget to check the appendices at the end of this book. They contain valuable additional resources which I hope you will find helpful.

With that being said, now I would like to encourage you to continue this journey of growth. From personal endeavors to relationships, it is emotional intelligence that can help navigate every situation with grace and positivity. Once we get attuned to our own emotions and inner self, we become a secure and confident person who doesn't see relationship challenges as a threat to their existence but as an opportunity to grow as an individual. So, stay optimistic, be open to change, and keep reflecting to preemptively prepare your mind and soul for what comes next.

Wishing you a future filled with a beautiful meaningful bond with your partner.

Thank you for being part of this journey!

If this book offered you valuable insights and helped you reshape your mindset to set your relationship on a more fulfilling path, then do please let me know through your kind feedback in a review and star rating on Amazon.

Your opinions are valuable, and I would also love to hear how your relationship has transformed.

This is the start of the rest of your love story.

Amazon US:

Amazon UK:

Appendix A

10 PRACTICAL TOOLS FOR BOOSTING YOUR EMOTIONAL INTELLIGENCE

It's time we go through the strategies and for you to pledge to practice them with consistency.

The Happy Couple Blueprint : Companion Workbook & Journal

This Workbook & Journal will help to support your development, keeping all your work from the book in one place for easy access and reference. It contains:

- Exercises and Questionnaires – try repeating these a few months after your initial work to see how the results might have changed.

- Affirmations – so important in helping you change your mindset.

- Your Journaling: to keep yourself on track. There are some useful prompts to help you keep on track.

- Tracking your core values and your goals.

Self-Awareness

To achieve this first component of emotional intelligence, you can practice:

- **Journaling, Morning Pages, and Self-Reflection:** Regularly journaling about your emotions, thoughts, and experiences helps you gain insights into your patterns and triggers.

- **Mood Tracking Apps:** Use apps that allow you to track your moods and emotional patterns over time, helping you identify trends and areas for improvement.

Self-Regulation

This second component of EI can be discovered through:

- **Mindfulness Meditation:** Practice mindfulness to stay present and manage stress. Apps like Headspace or Calm can guide you through meditation exercises.

- **Deep Breathing Techniques:** Incorporate deep breathing exercises to calm the nervous system and regulate emotions during moments of stress.

Motivation

It can be achieved through:

- **Identifying Values:** Clarify your values and align your goals with these values to create intrinsic motivation.

- **Goal Setting:** Set specific and achievable goals, both short-term and long-term, to stay motivated and focused on personal growth.

Empathy

Central to a meaningful relationship, you can develop empathy through:

- **Active Listening:** Practice active listening to truly understand your partner's perspectives. Repeat what you've heard to ensure you've accurately captured their feelings.

- **Perspective-Taking Exercises:** Put yourself in your partner's shoes to understand their emotions and motivations better. Consider different points of view in various situations.

Social Skills

There are endless ways to enhance your social skills, but the following two are the most effective ones:

- **Role-Playing:** Engage in role-playing scenarios to practice effective communication and conflict resolution skills.

- **Networking Events:** Attend networking events or social gatherings to improve interpersonal skills and build connections with diverse groups of people.

Recognizing Emotions

To read your emotions, you can try:

- **Emotion Recognition Games:** Use online games or apps that focus on recognizing facial expressions and body language associated with different emotions.

- **Daily Emotion Check-In:** Set aside time each day to check in with yourself and identify your current emotional state.

Conflict Resolution

The following techniques help to deal with the conflicts with a constructive approach:

- **Reflective Writing:** After a conflict, write about the experience, your emotions, and potential solutions in your journal. This helps in gaining clarity and finding constructive resolutions.

- **Role Reversal:** Imagine yourself in your partner's position to better understand their perspective and find common ground for resolution.

Positive Affirmations

They boost your morale, and keep you motivated:

- **Affirmation Cards:** Create or use affirmation cards with positive statements to reinforce a positive mindset and build self-confidence.

- **Gratitude Journal:** Regularly write down things you're grateful for to cultivate a positive outlook on life.

Feedback Seeking

Feedback offers valuable information about your behavior and mindset; you can evaluate it to change your attitude:

- **360-Degree Feedback:** Seek feedback from your partner to gain a well-rounded view of your strengths and areas for improvement.

- **Feedback Journal:** In your journal, record and reflect on feedback received, highlighting patterns and areas to focus on.

Appendix B

RESOURCES FOR FURTHER EXPLORATION

Emotional intelligence, self-awareness, empathy, and all the other topics we have touched on in this book, are quite diverse subjects in themselves. So, I would like to recommend you continue reading and developing an even stronger foundation of knowledge and understanding.

My Top Further Reading Recommendations

- "The Essential Beginner's Guide to Meditation and Mindfulness" by Rohini Heendeniya *(Improve Your Life Skills series)*

- "Emotional Intelligence: Why It Can Matter More Than IQ" by Daniel Goleman

- "Emotionally Focused Therapy for Couples" by Sue Johnson

- "Hold Me Tight: Seven Conversations for a Lifetime of Love" by Sue Johnson

- "The High-Conflict Couple: A Dialectical Behavior Therapy Guide to Finding Peace, Intimacy, and Validation" by Alan E. Fruzzetti

- "Nonviolent Communication: A Language of Life" by Marshall B. Rosenberg

- "The Relationship Cure: A 5-Step Guide to Strengthening Your Marriage, Family, and Friendships" by John Gottman

- "The Seven Principles for Making Marriage Work" by John Gottman and Nan Silver

- "Wired for Love: How Understanding Your Partner's Brain and Attachment Style Can Help You Defuse Conflict and Build a Secure Relationship" by Stan Tatkin

- "Attached: The New Science of Adult Attachment and How It Can Help You Find—and Keep—Love" by Amir Levine and Rachel Heller

Online Platforms

You can also use online platforms to learn about EI and relationships.

- Gottman Institute (gottman.com): It provides articles, videos, and resources based on the research of Dr. John Gottman, a renowned expert in the field of relationships.

- Psychology Today - Relationships Section (psychologytoday.com): It offers a wide range of articles and expert advice on various aspects of relationships and emotional well-being.

Podcasts

Some amazing podcasts that you can listen to and broaden your views or share with your partner include:

- "Where Should We Begin?" with Esther Perel: A podcast where therapist Esther Perel provides real, unscripted couples therapy sessions, offering insights into different relationship dynamics.

- "The Love, Happiness & Success Podcast" by Dr. Lisa Marie Bobby: covers topics related to love, relationships, and emotional health, providing actionable advice and expert interviews.

Websites and Blogs

Alternatively, you can also read the latest articles and blogs on the following:

- Greater Good Science Center: It provides research-backed articles on happiness, empathy, and emotional intelligence – www.greatergood.berkeley.edu.

- Mindful.org: It offers resources and articles on mindfulness, a key component of emotional intelligence – www.mindful.org.

Therapy and Counseling

The following are some online platforms which are just my suggestions. They connect individuals with licensed therapists for counseling on relationships and emotional well-being. You could also search for qualified therapists in your area as well.

- BetterHelp (www.betterhelp.com)

- Talkspace (www.talkspace.com):

REFERENCES

Axinn, William G.; Ghimire, Dirgha J.; Thornton, Arland; Barber, Jennifer S.; Fricke, Thomas E. (Thomas Earl); Matthews, Stephen; Dangol, Dharma; Pearce, Lisa; Smoller, Jordan W.

Bodenmann, G., Falconier, M. K., & Randall, A. K. (2019). Editorial: Dyadic coping. Frontiers in Psychology, 10, 1498. https://doi.org/10.3389/fpsyg.2019.01498

Cahn D. D., & Abigail, R. A. (2014). Managing conflict through communication (5th ed.). Pearson Education.

Chiu, M., Ghoh, C., Chung, G., & Choi, K. P. (2019). Multistressed families in Singapore: A focus on transnational families. Children and Youth Services Review, 101, 372–382. https://doi.org/10.1016/j.childyouth.2019.04.014

Dutcher, J. M., Creswell, J. D., Pacilio, L. E., Harris, P. R., Klein, W. M. P., Levine, J. M., Bower, J. E., Muscatell, K. A., & Eisenberger, N. I. (2016). Self-affirmation activates the ventral striatum. Psychological Science, 27(4), 455–466. https://doi.org/10.1177/0956797615625989

Gottman, J. M., & Levenson, R. W. (1992). Marital processes predictive of later dissolution: Behavior, physiology, and health. Journal of Personality and Social Psychology, 63(2), 221–233.

Gu, R., Jing, Y., Yang, Z., Huang, Z., Wu, M., & Cai, H. (2018). Self-affirmation enhances the processing of uncertainty: An event-related potential study. Cognitive, Affective, & Behavioral Neuroscience, 19(2), 327–337. https://doi.org/10.3758/s13415-018-00673-0

Khazova, S. A. (2020). Emotional intelligence as a resource for codependent women. The European Proceedings of Social and Behavioural Sciences. https://doi.org/10.15405/epsbs.2020.10.04.27

Kiełek-Rataj, E., Wendołowska, A., Kalus, A., & Czyżowska, D. (2020). Openness and communication Effects on relationship satisfaction in women experiencing infertility or miscarriage: A Dyadic approach. International Journal of Environmental Research and Public Health, 17(16), 5721. https://doi.org/10.3390/ijerph17165721

Notre Dame News. (2015, December 21). Parent touch, play, and support in childhood vital to well-being as an adult. https://news.nd.edu/news/parent-touch-play-and-support-in-childhood-vital-to-well-being-as-an-adult/

Reyes, M. R., Brackett, M. A., Rivers, S. E., White, M., & Salovey, P. (2012). Classroom emotional climate, student engagement, and academic achievement. Journal of Educational Psychology, 104(3), 700–712. https://doi.org/10.1037/a0027268

Rosenberg, M. B. (2003). Nonviolent communication: A language of life (2nd ed.). Puddle Dancer Press.

Wollny, A., Jacobs, I., & Pabel, L. (2020, 2020/01/02). Trait emotional intelligence and relationship satisfaction: The mediating role of dyadic coping. The Journal of Psychology, 154(1), 75–93. https://doi.org/10.1080/00223980.2019.1661343

Wrench, J. S., McCroskey, J. C., & Richmond, V. P. (2008). Human communication in everyday life: Explanations and applications. Allyn & Bacon; pg. 423.

Also By This Author

Improve Your Life Skills series

This book offers practical guidance to the beginner for starting and continuing a meditation practice and incorporating mindfulness into their daily routine. It will guide you in reducing tension and anxiety and building feelings of clarity, wisdom, and calm. Through mindfulness, you will learn how to live in the present moment, appreciate the beauty of life, and find meaning and purpose in your daily activities.

You will embark on a transformative journey that goes beyond mere belief, delving into the practical application of Buddhist principles and its timeless philosophy. This guide serves as a roadmap to an awakened life, where you can experience a profound sense of purpose, meaning, and interconnectedness. By embracing these philosophical teachings, you will unlock the secrets to wisdom and inner peace and live in harmony with yourself and the world around you.

Published by Phoenix ePublishing

The Prophet
by Khalil Gibran
A 20th century classic of beguiling and captivating inspirational poetry, frequently quoted over the past 100 years all over the world, to mark important occasions and celebrations.

Tales from Shakespeare
by Charles and Mary Lamb

The celebrated volume of 20 Shakespeare's most well known plays written in story form, the ideal way to get to know these timeless stories.

Little Women
by Louise May Alcott
The classic story of four sisters, beloved by generations of girls ever since, for its warmth, heart, and humor.

What Katy Did & What Katy Did At School
by Susan Coolidge

An evergreen classic, two books in one volume, the story of a feisty and unconventional 12-year-old girl, living in the 1870s. These books have been loved by generations of girls.

Made in the USA
Coppell, TX
24 April 2024